ORTHO'S All About

Kitchen
Remodeling

Project Editor: Karen K. Johnson
Writers: Larry Hodgson and John Riha
Illustrators: Rick Hanson, Shawn Wallace, and Tony Davis

Meredith® Books
Des Moines, Iowa

Ortho® Books
An imprint of Meredith® Books

Ortho's All About Kitchen Remodeling
Editor: Larry Erickson
Writer: John Riha
Art Director: Tom Wegner
Copy Chief: Catherine Hamrick
Copy and Production Editor: Terri Fredrickson
Contributing Proofreaders: Joan Fitzpatrick Bolin, Steve
    Hallam, Colleen Johnson
Electronic Production Coordinator: Paula Forest
Editorial and Design Assistants: Kathleen Stevens, Judy
    Bailey, Kaye Chabot, Treesa Landry, Karen Schirm
Production Director: Douglas M. Johnston
Production Manager: Pam Kvitne
Assistant Prepress Manager: Marjorie J. Schenkelberg

**Additional Editorial Contributions from
    Art Rep Services**
Director: Chip Nadeau
Designer: lk Design
Illustrators: Rick Hanson and Brad McKinney

Meredith® Books
Editor in Chief: James D. Blume
Design Director: Matt Strelecki
Managing Editor: Gregory H. Kayko
Executive Ortho Editor: Benjamin W. Allen

Director, Sales & Marketing, Retail: Michael A. Peterson
Director, Sales & Marketing, Special Markets:
    Rita McMullen
Director, Sales & Marketing, Home & Garden Center
    Channel: Ray Wolf
Director, Operations: George A. Susral

Vice President, General Manager: Jamie L. Martin

Meredith Publishing Group
President, Publishing Group: Christopher M. Little
Vice President, Consumer Marketing & Development:
    Hal Oringer

Meredith Corporation
Chairman and Chief Executive Officer: William T. Kerr

Chairman of the Executive Committee: E.T. Meredith III

Photographers
Laurie Black: 32
Stephen Cridland: 35BR
Edward Gohlich: 82T
Hedrich-Blessing Studios: 34
Jerry Howard/Positive Images: 14
Linda Mason Hunter: 27
Mark Lohman: 35T
Geoffrey Nilsen: 6, 7, 8, 9, 10, 11T, 13, 16T, 49B, 64, 92
Kenneth Rice: 11B, 48, 49T, 70T, 70B, 71, 80, 81L, 81R, 82B, 83T, 88T
Eric Roth: 22
Anita Sabarese: 39T
Rick Taylor: 4, 35M, 35BL, 67B
Robert Thien: cover
Jessie Walker: 46

All of us at Ortho® Books are dedicated to providing you
with the information and ideas you need to enhance your
home and garden. We welcome your comments and
suggestions about this book. Write to us at:
Meredith Corporation
Ortho Books
1716 Locust St.
Des Moines, IA 50309–3023

If you would like more information on other Ortho
products, call 800-225-2883 or visit us at www.ortho.com

Note to the Readers: Due to differing conditions, tools,
and individual skills, Meredith Corporation assumes no
responsibility for any damages, injuries suffered, or losses
incurred as a result of following the information published
in this book. Before beginning any project, review the
instructions carefully, and if any doubts or questions remain,
consult local experts or authorities. Because codes and
regulations vary greatly, you always should check with
authorities to ensure that your project complies with all
applicable local codes and regulations. Always read and
observe all of the safety precautions provided by
manufacturers of any tools, equipment, or supplies,
and follow all accepted safety procedures.

PLANNING 4

REMODELING BASICS 22

FLOORING 32

CABINETS 50

COUNTERTOPS 66

INSTALLING PLUMBING FIXTURES AND APPLIANCES 80

Careful planning ensures this modest kitchen has ample storage, plenty of light, generous work surfaces, and a pleasing blend of colors and textures.

PLANNING

What room works harder and requires more versatility than your kitchen? In addition to its traditional role as a place to prepare meals, it is a household gathering place and the host for family activities: We eat, socialize, do homework, plan business projects, play games, and talk on the telephone, all within the friendly confines of the kitchen. No wonder a kitchen remodeling is the major makeover project that American homeowners are most likely to undertake.

Any kitchen remodeling is an investment of your time and money, and it's important to manage this investment with careful planning. No matter what your level of do-it-yourself experience, your project will benefit from setting specific goals and having a thorough knowledge of the work involved. A good plan will help you stay on budget and make the most efficient use of your time.

Even small kitchen remodelings can be complex. For example, you can't replace a countertop without shutting off the water supply, removing the sink and faucet, and disconnecting the drain pipes. Larger projects may involve doing electrical work, resurfacing walls or ceilings, hiring subcontractors, and meeting legal obligations. Knowing every step will enable you to set a realistic time frame and have a clear expectation of costs.

USING A DESIGN PROFESSIONAL

If your kitchen goals are complex or if your design skills are limited, consider seeking the help of a kitchen designer. Certified Kitchen Designers have passed rigorous tests, administered by the National Kitchen and Bath Association (NKBA), which ensure they have a thorough knowledge of products and procedures. They usually work as independent contractors in association with architects and builders, or are allied with retailers.

Finding a good kitchen designer is similar to finding a good doctor or dentist—your best recourse is probably to seek the recommendations of family or friends. Pay close attention to the rapport you establish with the prospective designer. Your ability to achieve good communication will greatly affect the success of your project. Once you've narrowed your choices, ask to see finished projects so you can judge the quality of designs.

Another way to scout for competent professionals is by looking in local publications for features about kitchen remodelings. If you find a project you like, find out the name of the designer. Or visit local showhouses and model homes. If you plan to hire a remodeling contractor, ask for referrals for a designer. Contractors often have preferences based on successful past projects.

Kitchen supply retail shops, which usually offer a selection of cabinets, appliances, and finish materials, often have a kitchen designer on staff. You can find a list of them in the yellow pages of your telephone directory under Kitchen Cabinets & Equipment. If you make major purchases through a kitchen supply retailer, you may be able to obtain the complimentary services of the staff designer.

The better the designer understands what you want, the more likely you will obtain a good design. When meeting with your designer, bring along a file of photographs of your favorite kitchens clipped from magazines, a picture of the existing kitchen, any preliminary plans, and your budget requirements.

Kitchen designers can be flexible, and you can retain their services for all or part of the design work. They can check to see if your kitchen design is workable, provide a complete floor plan, specify materials, or oversee the entire remodeling job.

KITCHENS FOR TODAY

Crisp white cabinets paired with granite countertops and backsplashes bring comfortable elegance to this remodeled corridor kitchen.

The way Americans live is constantly changing, and often those changes are reflected in the design and use of kitchens. For example, personal time is increasingly precious, and we manage our time with quick-cooking microwave ovens, informal eating areas that permit fast access to food and tableware, and easy-to-clean features such as under-the-counter sinks. Kitchens increasingly are the site of activities. Families open up the kitchen to adjacent rooms or include a planning center that provides space for a computer and a desk to do homework.

You probably have several reasons for remodeling your kitchen. You may simply want to upgrade some materials or change the look of your existing space. Or, you might want to increase the total square footage of your kitchen and add a whole new arrangement of cabinets. The next few pages provide an overview of some of the most popular reasons people have for remodeling their kitchens. Some of these ideas may already have occurred to you, but others may provide fresh inspiration. Most of these cost-effective ideas are relatively easy to include in your kitchen design plans.

UPGRADING MATERIALS, APPLIANCES, OR FIXTURES

A kitchen remodeling project usually includes upgrading materials, surfaces, or appliances. If no structural changes are included, the project often is referred to as a facelift. Facelifts are the most popular type of kitchen remodeling. They hold their value better than many other home improvements, and most tasks are accomplished readily by a do-it-yourselfer with moderate building skills.

You can change the look of your kitchen dramatically without altering walls, floors, or cabinet configurations. You can repaint cabinets, add new cabinet hardware, replace a faucet, and install a new stove without ever swinging a hammer.

Even the most modest facelift will benefit from planning. Be sure to research all products you intend to purchase and understand their application or installation procedures. To replace appliances or fixtures, you should know the exact sizes and configurations needed. Know every step-by-step process before you begin. Establish a target budget and keep records of all expenditures. If you plan to use subcontractors or other professionals for some or all of the work, obtain two or three estimates before proceeding.

Many do-it-yourselfers recognize the value of turning to a professional for design help. Professionals have many years of experience visualizing changes and offer expertise in combining materials, textures, and colors. Often, a professional's efforts will save money over the life of a project by making efficient use of design time and identifying problems a homeowner might not anticipate. When the design is complete and all materials and appliances have been specified, the owner still can save money by strapping on a toolbelt and doing some or all of the work.

A second sink mounted in a large central island provides workspace for two. Note how both sinks are within easy reach of appliances.

TWO-COOK KITCHENS

Today, it's not unusual to have more than one member of the household contributing to meal preparation on a regular basis. This increased participation requires room for everyone to move about freely. According to guidelines established by the NKBA, a working aisle—a corridor where food preparation, cooking, or cleanup occurs— should be at least 42 inches wide in a standard kitchen. For a two-person kitchen the working aisle should be at least 48 inches wide. These are especially helpful guidelines when designing a kitchen that includes a center island. For most U-shape

arrangements, the inside edge of the legs of the U should be no less than 64 inches apart. For a two-cook kitchen, the minimum measurement should be 72 inches.

Counter space also should be increased. Each cook needs at least 3 feet of clear countertop, located at least 18 inches away from a shared sink or cooktop to avoid crowding others working there.

You won't have to double up on all appliances and equipment, but a second sink is a valuable addition for a kitchen with two cooks. Locate the second sink 6–9 feet from the primary sink so the cooks can create meals and clean up without getting in each other's way. A second sink will reduce the available counter area, so make sure there's enough to accommodate a second cook as outlined above.

A second sink doesn't have to be as large as the primary sink, but avoid the 16- to 20-inch "bar sinks," which aren't large enough to handle food preparation and cleanup chores. Be sure to outfit your second sink with a garbage disposer.

KITCHENS FOR TODAY
continued

EAT-IN KITCHENS

There's something cozy about gathering in the kitchen to eat, whether it's for a quick snack or an informal family dinner. It's also convenient—you only have to take a few steps to serve or clean up.

Spacious kitchen designs, of course, offer plenty of opportunity to add a table and chairs. But in more compact kitchens, a snack

A peninsula counter is a handy place for quick meals. This peninsula's two-level top fits diners as well as cooks. And it hides cooking and cleanup from the view of guests in the adjacent room.

counter or booth may fit best. Wherever you decide to place your eat-in area, you'll want to make sure it's not in a traffic corridor.

Accommodating a table and chairs depends on the available floor space and the number of people you'd like to seat. Plan 12–15 square feet of floor space for each person. A table and chairs for a family of four, for example, requires a minimum of 48 square feet. To have access to chairs, you need to allow a minimum of 32 inches from nearby walls to chair backs. To walk comfortably around the table for serving, there should be 44 inches from walls to chair backs. Make sure you take all of these measurements into account if you

plan to extend your table with leaves to allow for dinner guests.

Snack counters are a good way to increase the versatility of your counter space. Kids love the informality, and you'll find these counters a great place for casual chats and morning coffee. A peninsula design works well as a snack counter. Because peninsula countertops are often 36 inches across—larger than the standard 24 inches—there's plenty of room to include a snack counter.

To decide how many people your snack counter can serve, allow 21 inches of countertop length for each person. You'll need at least 24 inches of free space (depth) under the counter for knees and 12 inches between the bottom of the counter and the top of the seat. If you plan to use a standard 36-inch-high counter, for example, the seats of stools or chairs should be no higher than 23 inches. To fit over standard 30-inch-high bar stools, plan a snack counter that is 42–48 inches high.

An alcove, a notch in the wall, or a recessed window offer ideal locations for an eating booth. Or, you can simply place one against a flat wall. With fixed seating, a booth for four can fit into a snug 42×60-inch space.

To determine the size of the table, allow 21 inches of table length and 15 inches of width for each person. A table for four, with two benches facing each other, should be at least 30 inches wide and 42 inches long. With the table at 28–30 inches high, the booth benches, or banquettes, should be 18 inches high, including cushions. Position the banquettes so that the front edges fall 3–4 inches inside the edges of the table.

PLANNING CENTERS

Also called kitchen offices, planning centers are handy locations for completing correspondence, taking care of household bills, and doing homework. A planning center usually includes a computer, storage for office supplies, a telephone, adequate task lighting, and a small desk surface. Locating a planning center in the kitchen places it at the hub of family activities and makes it readily accessible to every member of the household.

Integrate a planning center by using the same cabinet and countertop style as the rest of your kitchen. The desk surface should be at least 42 inches wide and 30 inches high—

lower than the standard countertop height of 36 inches. The desk surface can be the same depth as a standard kitchen countertop depth of 24 inches. However, if your computer monitor takes up too much space to position a keyboard in front of it comfortably, install a slide-out keyboard tray under the countertop.

Store office supplies in nearby cabinets and drawers. If work surface space is at a premium, consider installing strip lights under upper cabinets for task lighting, a bulletin board for notes, and a wall-mounted telephone.

KITCHENS OPEN TO FAMILY ROOMS

Many people enjoy a kitchen that opens to a family room. The two rooms are natural hubs of family activity, and their close proximity invites sharing simple pleasures. Those in the family room can savor the sounds and aromas of meals being fixed, and can have easy access to snacks during TV time. And a kitchen feels cozier when it has views of comfortable

family room chairs or perhaps a fireplace. The arrangement is particularly good for entertaining, as it allows guests and hosts to mingle even during meal preparation.

During remodeling, the two rooms can be blended by removing interior partition walls. The spaces can then be set apart with a peninsula of lower cabinets or a cabinet island that provides storage without obstructing the view to either room. To establish a visual link, consider using similar flooring and wall colors in both rooms. Enhance this connection by installing cabinets in the family room of the same style and color as those in your kitchen. Furniture styles and upholstery fabrics in the family room should harmonize with those in the kitchen.

Before removing any wall, however, determine if it is structural. Structural walls support other elements of your home's frame and cannot be removed without transferring that load to a bearing beam. If you are unsure about whether an interior wall is structural or not, consult a contractor or architect.

To integrate with the surrounding kitchen, this planning center uses similar materials for doors, drawers, and work surfaces.

KITCHENS FOR TODAY
continued

A large window over the sink, recessed ceiling fixtures, and a skylight provide ample lighting.

Select skylights with operable shades so you can regulate sunlight and the amount of solar heat your kitchen gains. Skylights come in many sizes and with a variety of features, so it's a good idea to discuss your particular situation with a designer or knowledgeable retailer.

Any opening in a roof risks leakage, and the last thing you want in your beautiful new kitchen is water damage or even an occasional drip. It may be worthwhile to hire a professional to finish the installation.

If your remodeling project includes opening up walls, be sure to examine your existing lighting scheme. Now is a good time to add wiring and install lights to provide your kitchen with additional lighting flexibility. If you are rearranging the layout of your cabinets, you will want to install task lighting in your ceiling to provide coverage for any new countertop surfaces (*see pages 16–17 for lighting ideas*).

EXPANDING WITH LIGHT AND WINDOWS

Nothing makes a kitchen more appealing—and easy to work in—than plenty of light. Sometimes, the addition of a well-placed window or skylight is all that's needed to change the look of the entire room. Giving existing windows a new look, such as adding an arched top or replacing a bank of windows with a bay window, is another strategy for changing the appearance of your kitchen by providing architectural interest and increasing available daylight. Bay windows also gain space that can be used for plant shelving or, if the bay is big enough, a window seat.

Skylights gather large amounts of daylight and you won't have to disrupt existing wall cabinet configurations to install them. You'll need to have just a roof or unused attic space above the kitchen, of course. A fixed skylight is the least expensive type, but an operable one—the kind that opens and closes—provides wonderful ventilation.

ADDING STYLE WITH ARCHITECTURAL DETAILS

You can give your kitchen personality and style by including interesting details that are easy on your budget. A good strategy is to splurge on a few specific details that dress up your kitchen without dramatically increasing costs. For example, if you are installing a tile countertop, consider adding a few hand-painted tiles to dress up the field, or install a rope-mold edging to the top of the backsplash. Other ideas include:
■ Custom cabinet knobs and drawer pulls.
■ A cabinet mix that includes two or three fancy ones—such as a pair of glass-front upper cabinets or shelves at the end of a peninsula.
■ New crown molding.
■ An arch-top window over an old window.
■ An interesting chandelier or pendant fixture over an eating area.

By enclosing the standard roof trusses with drywall, the designer of this kitchen created a pattern of light and shadow overhead.

INSTALLING A GRILL UNIT AND VENT HOOD

Today's lifestyles emphasize healthy cooking and eating, and it has become increasingly popular to grill foods indoors. Most kitchens can be retrofitted with 30- or 36-inch cooktop units that include grill options.

Because grilling generates smoke, a ducted vent hood system is essential. Ducted vent hoods use a fan to inhale smoke and cooking odors from the cooktop area. The smoke is then channeled outdoors through metal ducts.

In retrofit situations, having the cooktop located near an outside wall makes installing the duct system easy. If the cooktop is not located at an outside wall, you will have to consider your options carefully. One solution is to run ductwork inside soffits. If there is space between the tops of your upper cabinets and the ceiling, you may be able to build soffits to conceal the ductwork. Existing soffits must first be examined to see if they offer room for ductwork or if they can be rebuilt to accommodate ducts. Another idea is to run the ducts inside upper cabinets. While this idea saves tearing apart walls or soffits, it sacrifices storage. Ductwork also can be installed in ceilings—if the joists run parallel to the direction you wish to run the ducts and there are no other obstructions, such as pipes or heating-and-cooling ducts.

Some kinds of cooktops include downdraft vent systems. You may prefer this type for installation in a peninsula or island where a ceiling-mounted vent hood will obstruct views. The challenges for installing the ductwork for a downdraft unit are similar to those of putting in the vent hood. In a peninsula, you can run ductwork inside lower cabinets at the expense of storage space. Or, you may be able to route ductwork between floor joists, providing there is enough room amid existing ductwork and pipes. Downdraft cooktop vents installed in islands can only be vented one way—through the floor.

SMALL KITCHEN LIVES BIG

Designing a compact kitchen can be a challenge, but there are ways to maximize space that will help your kitchen live up to its potential. The key is to simplify.

■ Rely on smooth lines and simple patterns to create an illusion of more space. Align appliances flush with cabinets for a continuous, unbroken plane. Reduce the number of visual elements by specifying simple cabinet styles with concealed hinges.

■ Employ a neutral or pastel color scheme and limit the number of colors. Keeping the hues of cabinets, walls, and flooring in close proximity helps create a feeling of expansiveness. Reserve bolder colors for simple accents such as cabinet hardware.

■ Eliminate clutter. Keep refrigerator surfaces bare. Display items atop cupboards rather than on counters. Keep counters clear by placing small appliances, recipe boxes, and spices behind cabinet doors.

A subtle cabinet enclosure makes this vent hood nearly disappear.

SETTING A KITCHEN REMODELING BUDGET

Costs are like helium balloons; they'll quickly soar out of reach if you don't maintain a firm grip on the bottom line. Creating a sound budget—and sticking to it—is essential to a successful project.

To set a budget, you need to figure out more than just how much money you'll spend. Equally important is knowing if your money will be spent wisely and if your plans will result in a good value. This is the first step toward creating a sound budget.

of both time and money. By carefully analyzing the condition of your kitchen, you may find that simple cosmetic changes are all that's needed to create a whole new look. For example, you may not be able to afford both tile countertops and new cabinets, but perhaps you can have the tile if you're willing to paint your old cabinets. The savings may allow you to splurge on special hardware to further upgrade the look of your cabinets.

YOUR SPENDING CAP

Start by finding out the value of your home and the average price of homes in your neighborhood. A real estate agent should be able to help you with an estimate. If your home is typical of houses in your area, the cost of your project generally shouldn't exceed 10 percent of the current estimated value. Anything more could be difficult to recover when you eventually sell your home.

For example, if the average value of homes in your neighborhood is $130,000 and your home is typical, a kitchen remodel costing more than $13,000 is unlikely to raise your home's value proportionately. Spending $45,000 may result in a wonderful kitchen but may not be a shrewd investment. From an investment standpoint, it's better to tailor your plans to the value of your house or consider buying another house instead.

Once you've determined the amount you're willing to spend, you should outline the scope of your project. Make a list of priorities and be prepared to make compromises. A complete renovation is a major commitment

SOURCES OF FUNDS

Where's the money going to come from? Ideally, the primary source should be your own savings. Using cash on hand avoids having to borrow and pay interest on a loan. You can also borrow from your whole life insurance policy or your retirement plan, such as a 401(k), although you must pay penalties for early withdrawal from your retirement plan.

If you decide to borrow money, you might consider seeking a loan from a relative. This can be a mutually beneficial opportunity, but it should not be treated casually. Use appropriate loan documents so there is no future confusion about the arrangement.

Your credit cards may provide easy access to cash, but the high interest rates associated with credit cards makes this a poor option for all but the most modest needs.

To secure a loan from a lending institution, you'll have to make an application that certifies you'll be able to pay back the amount you borrowed, plus interest. If applicable, you may be able to seek a loan from the Veterans

HIDDEN COSTS YOU NEED TO UNDERSTAND

You should have an understanding of labor costs and any "hidden costs" associated with your project. A new sink might cost $250, but then there are the costs of disconnecting plumbing and removing the old sink, as well as costs for installing the new sink and reconnecting pipes and wires. Adding a $100 garbage disposer might seem reasonable, but don't forget the cost of installing a new

electrical wall switch to control the unit. Remember that remodeling often reveals unanticipated problems, such as corroded pipes or rotten floorboards. When budgeting, it's a good idea to reserve 10 percent of your overall budget for unforeseen problems and other cost overruns.

To establish reasonable costs, ask for estimates from reliable professional contractors. If you need to,

you'll be able to analyze each part of the project to see where you might save money. One way is to do some of the work yourself. You'll save money, but you'll need enough free time and the right skills and tools to do the job. If your do-it-yourself skills are minimal, talk to your contractor about the possibility of completing tear-out and cleanup chores yourself.

Administration or the Federal Housing Administration. These organizations usually have loans available at rates lower than commercial lending institutions.

Many banks, credit unions, and other financial institutions have loans specifically for home improvement or construction that use your home as collateral. Shop around for loan prices before making a decision. Compare the length of the loan, how much is due each month, the interest rates, the total amount of interest paid over the course of the loan, and any additional loan fees.

You may be able to refinance your home or get a second mortgage to obtain the money for your remodel. Usually, the best type of loan depends on general economic conditions at that time. A qualified loan officer should be able to outline your options and help you make a decision about the type of loan that's best for you.

Budget-minded homeowners bought stock cabinets, standard white tile, and laminate countertops directly from a home center to minimize costs.

HOW MUCH WILL IT COST?

This chart lists various kitchen projects and their approximate costs. Estimates will vary according to your location and materials. Levels of difficulty are rated on a scale, with five (•••••) being the most difficult.

Remember that doing the work yourself is not a total savings over the contractor's cost. You'll undoubtedly need tools and far more time. Also, a contractor can offer guarantees against defects in workmanship. If you do the job improperly yourself, you may have to do it over or hire a professional to fix it.

REPLACE A SINK
Disconnect all plumbing, remove the old sink, and install a new, top-grade, double-bowl sink.
- Level of difficulty ••
- Do it yourself: $400
- Contractor's cost: $850

INSTALL AN ISLAND CABINET
Put in a new base cabinet with two doors, two drawers, and a maple butcher-block top.
- Level of difficulty •••
- Do it yourself: $500
- Contractor's cost: $800

INSTALL VINYL SHEET FLOORING
Pull baseboards, install plywood underlayment and 120 square feet of good-quality vinyl sheet flooring, paint, and install new baseboards.
- Level of difficulty ••••
- Do it yourself: $850
- Contractor's cost: $1,600

INSTALL CERAMIC TILE FLOORING
Put down plywood underlayment and about 120 square feet of good ceramic tile, all mortar, grout, and sealers.

- Level of difficulty •••
- Do it yourself: $650
- Contractor's cost: $1,250

PAINT KITCHEN WALLS
Brush on a primer coat and one coat of good-quality paint on about 500 square feet of wall, plus about 75 lineal feet of trim.
- Level of difficulty •
- Do it yourself: $60
- Contractor's cost: $450

INSTALL CUSTOM LAMINATE COUNTERTOP
Remove old countertop and install 25 linear feet of new laminate countertop with backsplash, mitered corners, and sink cutouts.
- Level of difficulty ••••
- Do it yourself: $180
- Contractor's cost: $900

ARRANGING THE SPACE

If you plan to rearrange your kitchen, or to tear it out and start over, consider how you will use the space. You should plan for efficiency and convenience, and provide for any special needs. If you enjoy baking, for example, plan an area for that activity. Make a list of priorities to help guide your decisions.

THE TRIANGLE

Studies from the 1950s revealed specific trends that would dictate how kitchens were designed for many years afterwards. Those studies indicated that efficiency could be increased if kitchens were arranged to minimize the steps taken between several key points—places for food preparation, cooking, and cleanup. This concept, often called "the kitchen triangle," is used widely today. Ideally, the perimeter of the triangle should be no less than 15 feet to avoid crowding and no more than 22 feet to save steps.

Those early studies also identified certain lifestyle patterns: Most women stayed home during the day, worked alone in the kitchen, prepared most meals with fresh ingredients, and stored some 400 items.

YOU'VE CHANGED

However, times have changed. More recently, the National Kitchen and Bath Association has identified the different lifestyle patterns in the American kitchen. Today, most couples work outside the home, share cooking duties, prepare packaged foods regularly, and store more than 800 items.

These shifting patterns require rethinking the concept of the kitchen triangle. A more contemporary view is to divide the kitchen into work centers that provide for specific culinary interests and allow more flexibility. Do two people in your family often cook together? You'll need two food preparation areas and possibly a second sink, with adequate floor space between these areas to permit two people to move about freely. Are there teenagers on the go? You might want to add a snack station—a tall counter with stools in close proximity to the refrigerator and microwave to allow quick-fix meals. Figure that each specialty area—baking area, snack center, second cleanup center, and desk —requires at least 36 inches of wall space.

THE PANTRY REVIVAL

Adding specialty items such as work centers or baking centers may require reallocating space that might otherwise go to cabinets, countertops, and shelves. One popular solution, if you have enough room, is to create a pantry. Popular in kitchens in the early 1900s, pantries provide a separate storage area for canned goods, bulk items, and little-used appliances and utensils. An ideal pantry has room for 10-inch shelves around the perimeter and a 32-inch-wide passageway that is at least 3 feet long. Pantries also need plenty of light. If possible, locate your pantry on an outside wall so you can have a window to provide daylight.

DESIGN INSIGHTS

Other kitchen-planning ideas to consider:
■ Conventional ovens that are separate from the cooktop can be placed outside the immediate work area with little inconvenience.
■ Serious cooks often favor having two ovens.
■ Locate pantries and refrigerators near the food preparation area. To prevent a door from getting in the way, place hinges on the side farthest from the food preparation area. For loading and unloading groceries, try to include at least 15 inches of countertop on the handle-side of the refrigerator.
■ The standard height for countertops, 36 inches from the floor, can be varied to suit the cooks. The maximum variance shouldn't exceed 2 inches. If you alter the height of your countertops, carefully consider what the changes will do to openings for appliances, such as a dishwasher, and to the structure of the lower cabinets.

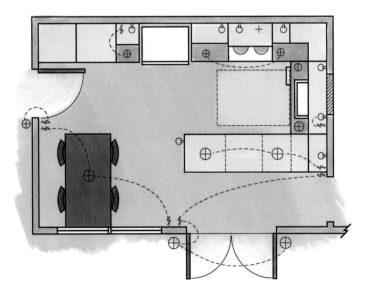

A

B

C

D

E

Although the design possibilities are endless, most kitchens are confined to these basic shapes:
A. The popular L-shape kitchen is illustrated again in perspective, **above**.
B. Corridor kitchens often appear in apartments.
C. Pass-through corridors, often found in older homes, have work centers on opposite sides but must deal with traffic.
D. This U-shape kitchen provides maximum space for work and storage.
E. Cooks in this U-shape kitchen must be prepared for traffic through the central space.
OPPOSITE: Every plan should include ideas for placement of lighting fixtures.

KITCHEN LIGHTING

A thoughtfully designed scheme for recessed lighting ensures that all kitchen work surfaces receive adequate illumination.

Well-planned lighting contributes to the efficiency and safety of your kitchen. Your lighting scheme should provide not only adequate general lighting but also illumination for specific tasks. If your kitchen will be extensively remodeled, make lighting a vital part of your plans. Even a simple modification—such as a row of strip lights to help illuminate a section of countertop—can brighten the prospect of working in your kitchen.

There are two types of room lighting:

■ AMBIENT LIGHT is soft, general light that spans an entire room. Ambient light is provided by windows or skylights, central ceiling fixtures, or perimeter soffit lights that direct light upwards to reflect off the ceiling.

AMBIENT LIGHT

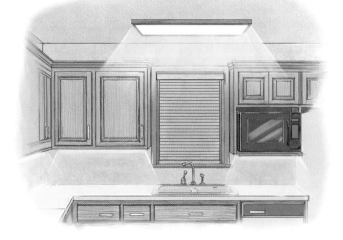

■ TASK LIGHTING—a strong beam focused on a specific location—is often placed directly above sinks, food preparation areas, and cleanup centers. Specialty areas such as baking centers or desks need task lighting that is bright but not harsh.

The amount of ambient lighting that you need depends on a number of factors, including the room's height and color. Bright tones reflect light and require less general illumination; dark tones absorb light and require more.

GUIDING LIGHT

Provide at least 100 watts of incandescent light or 75 watts of fluorescent light for each 50 square feet of floor space.

During the day, windows are the primary source of ambient light. Generous windows help make a kitchen feel airy, cheerful, and spacious, but it's necessary to balance your need for windows with your need for upper cabinet storage space. If your kitchen space is limited, you can increase light by replacing existing windows with taller versions, or by

TASK LIGHTING

adding a fixed, arch-top window over an existing window. Either strategy adds a significant amount of daylight but doesn't require sacrificing additional wall space. And you add an interesting architectural detail. You'll have to be careful, however. Installing a different-size window requires changing the wall framing by moving the horizontal support, known as the header, over the window. If your walls are short, you may not have room to raise the header high enough.

Another way to add daylight is to install skylights, which don't interfere with cabinet configurations. If you increase the amount of daylight your kitchen receives, be sure that windows and skylights can be shaded to prevent them from overheating the space.

Indirect lighting can supplement the ambient light from your central ceiling fixtures. Bulbs located in soffits and aimed upward to reflect off the ceiling provide soft, sculpted light that is especially beautiful.

Fixtures for task lighting create

UNDERCABINET LIGHTING

concentrated, high-intensity beams that can be directed at specific work centers. Recessed down lights, track lights, hanging pendant lights, and undercabinet strip lights are all examples of task lighting fixtures. Each work center should be lighted with a minimum of 100–150 watts of incandescent light or 40–50 watts of fluorescent light. For efficiency, the lighting for each work center should be controlled by its own wall switch.

Ceiling-mounted task lighting cannot effectively illuminate the area underneath upper cabinets. The solution is to install strip lighting. Strip lighting, made specifically to be installed under upper cabinets, usually has a thin profile that allows the fixture to be nearly hidden. Fluorescent lighting is a good choice for this type of task lighting. The tube should be two-thirds the length of the counter it lights and provide about 8 watts of power per foot of counter. For example, a 6-foot run of counter calls for a 4-foot fluorescent tube of 48 watts.

SOFFIT LIGHTING

Each type has its advantages:

■ INCANDESCENT light has a warm glow that enhances yellow and red colors and complements skin tones. Incandescent fixtures are available in a variety of styles, and the bulbs are inexpensive and easy to change. One great advantage of incandescent lighting is that it can be placed on a dimmer switch (sometimes called a rheostat), which allows you to vary the amount of light.

■ FLUORESCENT lights are energy efficient, lasting up to 20 times as long as incandescent bulbs. They produce up to four times as much light as incandescent bulbs of the same wattage, so fewer fixtures are required. Advancements in fixture design have shortened the "hesitation period"—that momentary pause between flipping the switch and getting full illumination.

■ HALOGEN lights provide powerful illumination in a small size. They're up to three times as bright as comparable incandescents and last twice as long. Their compact design allows installation of tiny, unobtrusive fixtures. Halogens burn at high temperatures. So, for safety reasons, they are best installed as ceiling-mounted task lights.

KITCHEN LAYOUT

Remodeling can be expensive and time-consuming. That's why it's so important to plan carefully and give yourself the opportunity to change your mind. One of the best ways to accomplish your goals is to create a floor plan on paper. With the aid of paper templates for cabinets, appliances, and furniture, you can move walls and arrange your kitchen until the design is perfect.

To help visualize your final kitchen layout, use the symbols shown on the following pages to place appliances, cabinets, and seating. Make an accurate sketch of your kitchen floor plan on graph paper using a ¼-inch scale (¼ inch equals 1 foot). Include all windows and doors. Then photocopy the symbols, cut them out, and arrange them in trial configurations. Allow for the distances between items, widths of corridors, and door openings that are described on these pages.

A VISUAL AIDE

To begin, measure your kitchen and any other rooms affected by your remodeling plans. Sketch the walls of your kitchen on a piece of graph paper, using a scale of ¼ inch equals 1 foot. This is a good scale for beginning to visualize changes, and it allows you to use the templates provided on these pages. Note the exact locations of electrical outlets, wall switches, lighting fixtures, doors, windows, and plumbing. When you're finished, it's a good idea to double-check all measurements for accuracy. At this point, you might want to create several photocopies of your sketch. That way, if one becomes damaged, you won't have to redraw the layout. Then you're ready to begin designing.

To use the templates, either photocopy or trace them, then cut out the shapes. Color makes the shapes easier to see and arrange.

DESIGN TIPS

As you design and arrange the elements, keep these layout tips and safety factors in mind:

■ To conserve costs, locate sinks and other plumbing fixtures along the same wall as they were before. That way, you can use the supply, drain, and vent stack systems without expensive alterations.

■ Provide at least 48 inches between appliances or counters that face each other.

■ Avoid having two doors, such as the doors of an oven or dishwasher, open directly toward each other (or having them too close together at an inside corner).

■ A U-shape kitchen should have at least 60 inches between the legs of the U. For two cooks, allow at least 72 inches.

■ Allow at least 42 inches of clearance on all sides of an island or peninsula.

■ Put tall units, such as a refrigerator, pantry, or broom closet, at the end of a counter rather than in the middle.

■ Design inside corners with care. Doors and drawers should not open into one another. Make allowances at corners for hardware and other protruding surfaces. Outfitting a corner with double-hinged corner doors or a lazy-susan unit is a good way to solve corner problems.

■ Design the kitchen so work areas are isolated from the traffic flow to other rooms.

■ Keep the cooktop away from windows and doors that swing over the cooking surface.

■ Provide counter space on both sides of the cooktop so pot handles do not hang over the edge.

■ Avoid storing frequently used items where you must reach over the cooktop to get them.

■ Be sure cooktop controls are child proofed adequately for your family's needs.

■ Provide separate storage for sharp knives, beyond the reach of children.

■ Plan for a smoke detector, fire extinguisher, and only ground fault circuit interrupter (GFCI) outlets within 6 feet of the sink.

Once you have settled on a design, finalize your decisions with a master plan that indicates all changes and new installations. Don't use the templates. Instead, draw everything directly onto the plan. If you are working with a contractor or subcontractors, a final plan will help communicate your ideas and make sure everything is done according to your specifications. Make several copies of your final plan so you can distribute them to everyone who needs them.

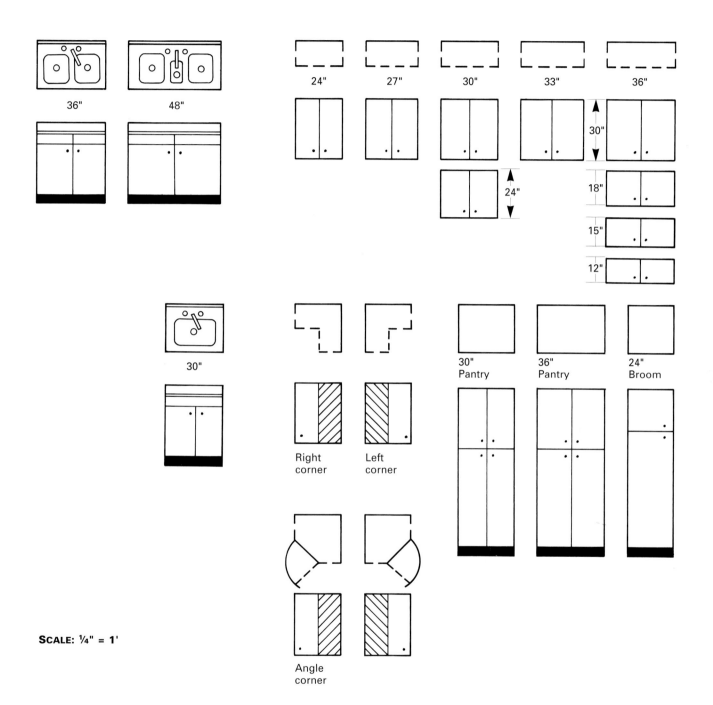

36"

48"

24"   27"   30"   33"   36"

30"

24"

30"

18"

15"

12"

30"

Right corner   Left corner

30"
Pantry   36"
Pantry   24"
Broom

Angle corner

SCALE: ¼" = 1'

KITCHEN LAYOUT
continued

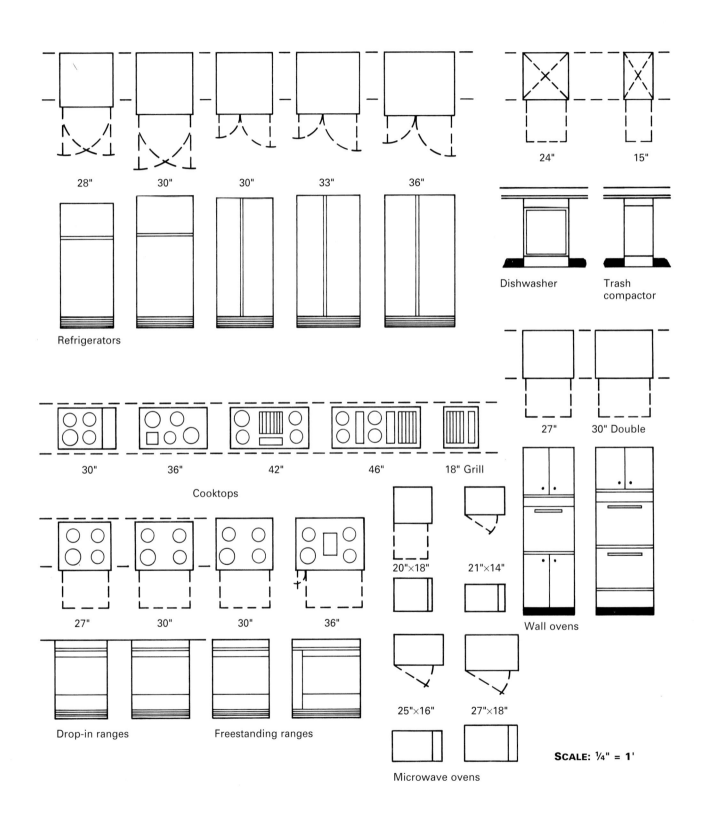

28" 30" 30" 33" 36"

24" 15"

Refrigerators

Dishwasher Trash compactor

30" 36" 42" 46" 18" Grill

Cooktops

27" 30" Double

27" 30" 30" 36"

20"×18" 21"×14"

Wall ovens

Drop-in ranges Freestanding ranges

25"×16" 27"×18"

Microwave ovens

SCALE: ¼" = 1'

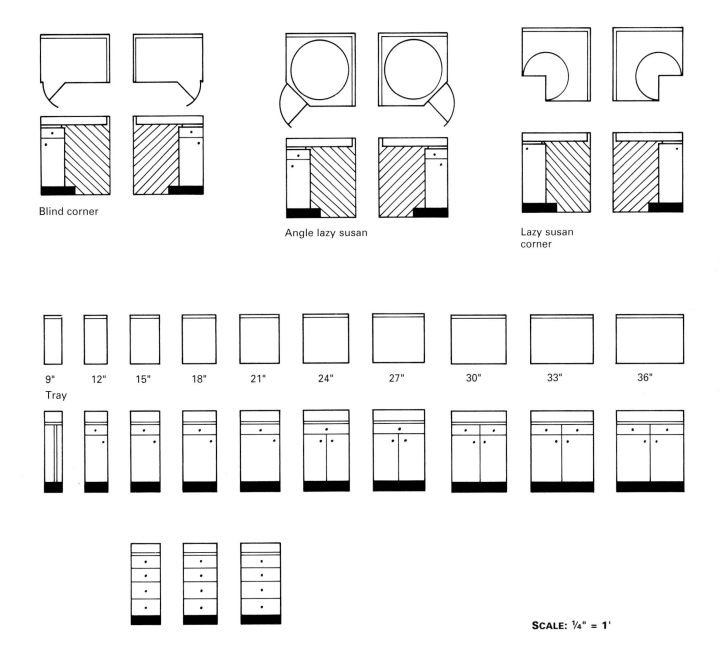

Blind corner

Angle lazy susan

Lazy susan corner

9" 12" 15" 18" 21" 24" 27" 30" 33" 36"

Tray

SCALE: ¼" = 1'

REMODELING BASICS

No matter how large or small your project, careful planning can prevent costly mistakes. If your remodeling includes moving walls or increasing the space, you'll need to acquire construction drawings and permits, understand local zoning ordinances and variances, and know how to specify materials. If you are using subcontractors to do all or part of the work, you'll need to know how to communicate effectively and how to set up contracts that work for everyone.

In order to place a window over the sink in their newly remodeled kitchen, these homeowners had to install a new header in the wall framing.

OBTAINING PERMITS

Most communities require building permits before construction begins. Usually the homeowner can apply for the permit, but some cities issue permits only to licensed contractors. Check with local building and zoning commissions about the procedure.

If you manage your project, you'll need to present detailed plans to obtain permits. If major structural work is involved, these plans should be completed by an architect or bear the approval stamp of a structural engineer. If your project includes substantial new plumbing, electricity, or foundation and framing, local authorities will check at various stages to be sure it meets codes. These inspections ensure the home's safety.

If general contractors do the work, they will have the responsibility of obtaining permits and making sure the construction passes inspections.

HOW TO SURVIVE REMODELING

Living without a kitchen is difficult. Keep these tips in mind to make the experience less stressful.
■ One of the best ways to maintain sanity is to keep the project site picked up and the house clean. Maintain normalcy wherever possible.
■ Set up a temporary kitchen (*see tips on page 24*).
■ Start and end your project with a sense of humor. If stress runs high, try to take the family on short escapes; an overnight trip or a weekend away can seem like a vacation.

HIRING PROFESSIONALS

If you hire professionals to help you complete the work, you have two options:
■ Act as your own project manager and hire subcontractors (electricians, plumbers, painters, and other specialists) to do specific jobs.
■ Hire a general contractor to oversee the entire job and to hire subcontractors for you. Either way, you can do some of the work yourself, as long as you communicate your intentions to your general contractor and specify your role in the signed contract.

To hire competent professionals, seek recommendations from friends or trusted professionals you have worked with before. Seek bids on your project from several sources, and check their references.

If you plan to act as project manager and hire subcontractors, you'll be responsible for obtaining permits, setting schedules, and checking the quality of the work. Keeping within your budget will largely depend on how you perform this challenging role.

If you hire a general contractor, your primary responsibility will be to establish good communications and to ensure the quality of the relationship by insisting on a well-written contract that is comprehensive and fair.

CLUES TO IDENTIFY A BEARING WALL

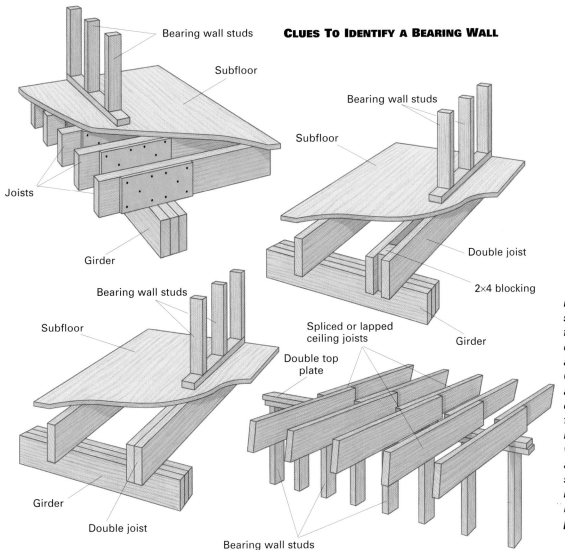

Bearing wall studs

Subfloor

Joists

Girder

Bearing wall studs

Subfloor

Double joist

2×4 blocking

Girder

Bearing wall studs

Subfloor

Spliced or lapped ceiling joists

Double top plate

Girder

Girder

Double joist

Bearing wall studs

Knowing how to strengthen floor framing is essential before adding new walls. Generally, girders and floor joists can be doubled or tripled in width to receive the extra weight. Consult an architect or structural engineer before beginning a major remodeling project.

YOUR CONTRACT IS YOUR ASSURANCE OF SATISFACTION

A good and equitable contract—one that is fair to all parties—should include these points:

■ Stipulate that all permits are to be obtained by the contractor and all work done according to governing building codes.

■ Specify start and completion dates and a detailed schedule. Specify penalties (if any) if the work is not performed as outlined.

■ Make a clear delineation between the contractor's duties and your own.

■ Specify the work you plan to do.

■ List materials that you will supply.

■ Require appropriate insurance coverages, such as liability and workers compensation.

■ Establish a payment schedule corresponding to key completion dates. Specify penalties (if any) if payments are not made as outlined.

■ Include a provision for the contractor to supply lien releases from all subcontractors and suppliers before final payment is made.

■ Set requirements for final payment, including final inspection by the building inspection department and a certificate of completion signed by you and the architect (if applicable). The date for final payment should include a 30-day waiting period to make sure you are satisfied with the work.

■ Specify procedures for

communication when more than one professional is involved.

■ Provide for change orders and contingencies.

Change orders occur if you want to alter details after the contract is signed. For example, you might opt for a tile backsplash instead of the laminate previously specified. This request must be made in writing and approved with the general contractor's signature.

Contingencies are surprises that crop up along the way. Opening up a wall, for example, may reveal termites. Outlining procedures for contingencies in your contract will help resolve unexpected problems.

DISMANTLING GUIDE

Taking apart a kitchen is the first step toward making a new one. It doesn't require a lot of expertise, but it must be done with care and common sense. It's a good job for the homeowner who doesn't have building trade skills but who would like to contribute labor to the project to save costs.

If you hire a general contractor, make your intentions clear and have your role described in the contract. Your contractor should be able to give you valuable advice about the dismantling process, what tools are required, and how to do the job safely.

Dismantling a kitchen is not necessarily a vigorous demolition with a sledgehammer and crowbar. Rather, it is a well-planned, step-by-step process that proceeds cautiously. If you plan on moving walls and making other structural changes, your primary objective should be to do the job safely. For that reason, usually the dismantling process requires more time and less brute force.

Dismantling is done generally in this order: appliances and fixtures, countertops, cabinets, ceilings and walls, and flooring. In all instances, you need to be aware which of your home's systems will be affected by the dismantling and take precautions. For example, if you are removing a sink, make sure the water supply to the faucet is turned off. Similarly, removing drywall probably means taking off switch plates or outlet covers. If so, power should be shut off at the electrical panel. Removal of electrical fixtures and wires, plumbing, or duct work should always proceed with your safety in mind.

If the kitchen project includes adding on new space, usually the shell for the addition can be framed up and closed in before you open up walls and disrupt your kitchen. Make sure there is a door or opening in the addition that is large enough to accommodate the removal of old cabinets and debris and the delivery of bulky items.

TEMPORARY RELIEF

Remodeling your kitchen undoubtedly will disrupt your domestic routine. Depending on the extent of your plans, your kitchen could be unavailable for days, weeks, or even months. To compensate, you'll need to create a temporary kitchen that allows for food preparation and cleanup.

Plan for a temporary kitchen before you begin demolition. Choose a space that will minimize inconvenience by locating temporary facilities near a bathroom, laundry, wet bar, or other sink. You'll need countertop space (a table will do) and a refrigerator. Plan to use a minimal number of cooking utensils, dishes, and silverware; create a storage area for these items.

Use space-saving cooking appliances such as a microwave oven, hot plate, and toaster oven. Set up cooking appliances in an area that has access to windows for ventilation and is away from curtains and other flammable materials. Your temporary kitchen should be equipped with a smoke detector and a fire extinguisher. If the weather is good,

consider using an outdoor grill or camp stove for cooking.

Be wary of overloading circuits in rooms not intended for use as kitchens. Appliances such as toaster ovens can draw a lot of electrical power, so try to use only one appliance at a time. Be sure that three-pronged cords are plugged into grounded outlets.

After you have set up your temporary kitchen, pack up all items in areas that are affected by the remodeling. Label cartons clearly, and store them in a convenient place where you can access items if needed.

Be prepared to employ several strategies to relieve the pressure of an extended project. In addition to your temporary kitchen, you might eat more often in restaurants, schedule regular meals with family and friends (and share costs), and stay a few days in a nearby hotel. Other options include borrowing or renting a recreational vehicle with built-in cooking and cleanup facilities, or taking an extended trip.

TOOLS FOR DISMANTLING

Dismantling the kitchen can be done easily and safely with the right tools. Most tasks require only basic hand tools, but they should be of good quality and used properly. Buying a quality hand tool is an investment that will last many years. Basic dismantling tools include:

■ hammer with a ripping claw and a steel or fiberglass handle
■ utility knife and extra blades
■ flat pry bar
■ 3-inch-wide putty knife
■ hacksaw (a mini-hacksaw, designed for use in tight spaces, is recommended also)
■ 8-point crosscut handsaw
■ 10-inch adjustable wrench
■ adjustable pliers
■ screwdrivers with flat-blade and Phillips heads
■ simple voltage tester to be sure electricity is turned off
■ flat shovel for loading debris
■ and a wheelbarrow for carrying equipment and removing debris.

Depending on the extent of your remodeling, you may need more specialized tools, such as side cutters for cutting wires, pipe wrenches for dismantling plumbing, and a basin wrench for removing the large nut that connects the drainpipe to the sink. Helpful power tools include a ⅜-inch drill with screwdriver bits for driving or removing screws (a cordless model is convenient) and a reciprocating saw with a variety of blades for cutting wood, metal, plastic laminates, and nails. Necessary safety equipment includes gloves, goggles, dust masks, work boots, and hard hats.

Use a voltage tester on receptacles and fixtures to ensure that the current is turned off before making any changes to the electrical system.

DEALING WITH TRASH

Your project probably will generate a lot of trash, especially during the dismantling phase. You have three options:

■ Haul everything away as it is removed, which requires a pickup truck or trailer and makes demands on your time.

■ Create a debris pile on your property and have it removed periodically by an independent trash service.

■ Rent a commercial steel debris box. Companies that rent debris boxes will empty the contents at regular intervals.

Whatever method you choose, insist on a clean building site at the end of the day—trash picked up, sawdust swept, and tools stored in secure locations. Clean building sites are safer for workers and homeowners, and are a courtesy to the neighborhood.

KEEPING IT ALL CLEAN

Keeping dust and debris out of your home is an important consideration throughout the project. Before you begin work, seal off doorways and passageways that open toward the remodeling. Shut any doors that can stay closed for the duration of the project and seal the edges with duct tape. If a door must be used, tape a piece of cloth along the bottom edge to block dust. Tape 4-mil plastic over passageways. If a passageway must be used regularly, apply two sheets of plastic that overlap about a foot at the middle. Tape the top and outside edges, but leave the middle free to accommodate traffic. Clear plastic allows workers to see if anyone is on the other side. In nearby rooms, drape sheets over furniture to shield them from dust.

Keep workers out of your living areas. If they need access to parts of your home, establish traffic routes and define boundaries. Remove wall art or breakable items from traffic routes.

SAFETY AND SECURITY

No work is successful if an injury occurs. To keep your project free from injuries, always observe these safe work habits:

■ Don't force objects when dismantling them. Let the tool do the work. If an item is especially stubborn, examine it carefully to see if another strategy can be used. Often, removing an unseen screw or other fastener is all that's needed to proceed easily.

■ Use safe lifting techniques. Use your legs instead of bending your back, keep a firm footing, and avoid twisting your back as you hold heavy objects.

■ Remove nails from boards or hammer over the nails before you toss lumber onto the debris pile.

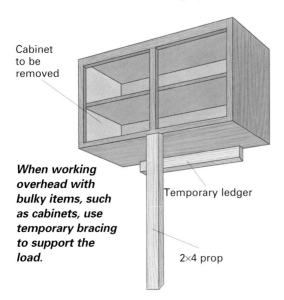

Cabinet to be removed

Temporary ledger

When working overhead with bulky items, such as cabinets, use temporary bracing to support the load.

2×4 prop

INSPECTION SCHEDULE

FOUNDATION
Check: Trench, forms, rebar
When: Before pouring concrete

UNDER FLOOR
Check: Floor frame, utility lines
When: Before installing subfloor

ROUGH PLUMBING
Check: Pipe sizes and fittings
When: Before framing is inspected or walls are covered

ROUGH WIRING
Check: Wire size, boxes, bends
When: Before framing is inspected or walls are covered

ROUGH MECHANICAL
Check: Ducts, flues, gas lines
When: Before framing is inspected or walls are covered

FRAMING
Check: Lumber grade and size, spans, connections, sheathing
When: Before walls are insulated or covered

INSULATION
Check: Thickness, joints, cracks
When: Before wallboard goes on

INTERIOR WALLS
Check: Wallboard nailing pattern (may not be required)
When: Before joints are taped

FINAL INSPECTION
Check: Electrical and plumbing fixtures, window glass, stairs
When: After completion

DISMANTLING GUIDE
continued

■ Wear a dust mask when cutting, sanding, or cleaning up.

■ Avoid working when you are tired or distracted. Be especially careful at the end of the day, when fatigue adds to the danger.

■ Use power tools with care. Have safety guards in place, wear goggles, and do not wear loose clothing. Keep cords away from traffic, and always use grounded plugs and outlets.

■ Turn off all utilities before you work on any appliance or remove wall or ceiling coverings. Most gas or propane appliances have shutoff valves, but you should know the location of the main shutoff valve in case you need to turn it off quickly. If you must turn off gas to the entire house, the pilot lights for your remaining appliances, such as the furnace and water heater, will go out. When the gas is turned back on, the pilot lights must be relit, unless they are equipped with electronic ignition devices. It's a good idea to have a service representative from your utility company come out to turn the gas back on whenever you disconnect gas appliances.

■ Turn off circuit breakers or disconnect fuses that serve the wiring where you will be working. Cover the breakers with tape to warn others that the current has been turned off intentionally. After turning off the current, use a voltage tester to check electrical outlets or fixtures that you plan to work around. If you are uncertain about disconnecting utilities, get professional help.

■ Notify your insurance agent about the construction work being done at your home— especially if you plan to enlist the help of family or friends. Be sure your policy covers any accident that may occur.

■ Demolition work often involves removing doors, windows, and even entire walls. Plan to secure these openings at the end of the work day. One way is to cover the openings with ⅜-inch plywood. Fix the plywood in place with 6d duplex nails. Duplex nails have two heads, one above the other. The first head will hold the plywood securely. The second protrudes above the surface of the plywood so that the nail can be pulled easily with a crowbar or claw hammer.

REMOVING WALLS AND CEILINGS

Getting rid of unwanted walls or ceiling materials isn't difficult, but it can be messy and time consuming. During demolition, immediately remove debris from the construction zone. Piles of old lumber and broken drywall are safety hazards.

Two types of residential walls are common:

■ **NONBEARING WALLS**—merely floor-to-ceiling partitions—can be removed without structural considerations.

■ **BEARING WALLS** support parts of your house—joists and other walls. Bearing walls cannot be removed without first providing other supports to carry the load.

If you are unsure about whether your walls are bearing or non-bearing, consult a builder or architect and seek advice about the construction of temporary supports.

WARNING: LEAD PAINT AND ASBESTOS

Occasionally, houses contain hazardous materials that must be removed properly so that they don't pose a health hazard. Houses built before 1978 may have been painted with lead-based paints. Sanding this type of paint creates dust that can cause health problems if it is inhaled. If you plan to sand or cut painted surfaces that you suspect have been covered with lead-based paints, you should contact an environmental assessment company or a company that specializes in lead paint inspection and testing. Look in the Yellow Pages of your phone book under "Lead Detection & Removal." These companies can test painted surfaces and give you an estimate for removal. For safety, wear a dust mask when cutting or sanding any painted surface.

Prior to 1975, asbestos was a popular material for fireproofing. A whitish-gray material similar to crumbly cardboard, asbestos was used to encase water heaters and to insulate hot water pipes. In older lighting fixtures, a small sheet of asbestos was often inserted between the bulb and the top of the fixture as insulation. It was also used in siding shingles and floor tiles. By itself, asbestos is not dangerous. But if it is disturbed, as often happens during a renovation project, tiny fibers can come loose from the asbestos sheets. If inhaled, these fibers pose a significant health risk. If you suspect asbestos materials, contact an environmental assessment company or a company that specializes in asbestos removal. Look in the Yellow Pages of your phone book under "Asbestos Abatement" or "Asbestos Consulting & Testing."

For more information on professionals or issues of environmental concern, contact your state, county, or local department of hazardous waste management, state health officials, or the federal agency of pollution control.

Demolition is dirty work and can produce lots of debris. Take the time to clean up the work site thoroughly at least once each day. An exhaust fan perched in a window will make cleanup easier and make demolition less stressful.

WHERE TO START: Begin wall and ceiling demolition by removing all trim. If removed carefully, trim can be reused. Score along the edges of the trim with a utility knife to break any paint bond. Beginning at outside corners, gently pry off the trim with a flat pry bar. Once an end is lifted, you may find it helpful to work with two tools—a flat pry bar and the claw end of a hammer. Use one tool to hold the trim away from the wall while you work the other tool behind the trim. After the pieces are removed, pull nails out through the back of the trim with pliers. If you try to hammer nails out through the front, you will likely splinter the front of the trim piece, rendering it useless. Number each piece on its back so later you will know where it goes.

CUT THE POWER: To remove wall or ceiling coverings, such as drywall, first turn off the electricity to that portion of your home. Check all receptacles and light fixtures with a voltage tester before proceeding. Remove all cover plates from switches and receptacles. If the wall contains plumbing, you will have to turn off the water supply.

To remove drywall, first score all wall and ceiling corners with a utility knife. Then, hammer or cut holes between studs or joists, taking care not to damage any pipes or wires behind the drywall. Insert a pry bar into the hole, and pull the drywall toward you. Most likely, drywall nails and screws will remain in the studs or joists and will have to be removed separately.

WORKING OVERHEAD: Be cautious when removing ceiling coverings. Always wear a hard hat and goggles. Work slightly in front of yourself, not directly overhead, but take care not to overextend your reach. Make sure ladders are firmly set.

After the wall coverings are off, you can remove the framing members. First, remove old wiring and plumbing. If you plan to reuse the same circuit wiring, cap the wire ends with electrical wire nuts and tape the wire nuts in place with electrical tape. Roll up the loose wire so it will not be damaged during reconstruction. Old plumbing will have to be removed. You will need to unscrew or cut the old plumbing at a point where it does not intrude on the reconstruction. At that point, supply pipes should be fitted with caps so that the water service can be restored for the duration of the project.

Lumber that is not broken or damaged during the dismantling process can be reused. Check old lumber for nails or other fasteners and remove them. Store old lumber flat so it will not warp. Prevent damage from moisture by placing scrap boards under lumber piles to keep the wood from coming in contact with the soil or damp concrete garage floors.

ROUGHING-IN THE SPACE

After demolition, you may need to do additional work called "roughing-in" to prepare for installations of new materials and appliances. The process includes framing walls, putting in subfloors, and installing water supply lines, vent stacks, and electrical cable and boxes in open walls.

No matter the extent of your involvement, familiarity with the process will help you plan your time and budget more precisely. If you hire a general contractor, knowing how a space is roughed-in will ensure clear communication when you discuss progress, make decisions, and plan change orders.

If the project involves adding space, the foundation can be built and the shell framed and closed in before you open up the wall and disrupt the existing kitchen. Remember to leave an opening large enough so old cabinets and debris can be removed easily and bulky new items, such as appliances, can be taken inside. If plumbing, wiring, or duct work will run under the floor, it must be installed and inspected before you apply subflooring over the joists. The exceptions are additions with basements big enough that an inspection can be made from below. Any plumbing vents, chimneys, flues, or ventilating ducts that go through the roof must be installed before the roofing goes on so that they can be flashed properly.

ROUGH FRAMING

Kitchen framing uses standard construction methods and a few special techniques. Be sure to take these into account when you are planning and budgeting the project.

FLOORS: If you want a ceramic tile floor, the material you use for your subfloor should not be less than 1¼ inches thick. You may use two layers of subflooring, such as ¾-inch plywood covered with ½-inch plywood, as long as the total thickness is at least 1¼ inches. This creates a stiff floor that prevents movement and reduces the chance of cracks appearing in the grout. Cementitious backer board, made especially to be applied under ceramic tile, is an excellent subfloor material. However, it is heavy, requires special tools for cutting, and is more expensive than plywood.

WALL BLOCKING: Blocking—short lengths of framing lumber—is installed between wall studs to stabilize framing and, in the event of a fire, to help prevent flames from migrating up the spaces between the studs. Blocking also provides a nailing surface for certain kinds of installations. For example, blocking should be applied between the studs where the tops of the cabinets will be aligned. This permits the cabinets to be readily screwed into place. For cabinet blocking, use 2×8 or 2×10 lumber nailed with the flat surface (the 8- or 10-inch dimension) placed vertically.

WING WALLS: Short walls 2–3 feet long often are used to enclose a refrigerator, define an alcove, or terminate a row of cabinets. If the wing wall extends to the ceiling, it can be framed like any stud wall, with the top plate nailed into the ceiling joists or into blocking set between the ceiling joists.

Sometimes a wing wall is designed to reach only part way to the ceiling to create a feeling of openness and to admit more light. Because a partial wing wall has no support along its top, other means must be used to stabilize it. A fixed corner cabinet, shelf, built-in seat, or adjacent countertop can be used to brace the wing wall. Other methods of stabilizing wing walls include using screws instead of nails to frame the wall, a method that creates especially tight joints. You also may cover the wall with thicker drywall (⅝ inch instead of the more common ½ inch) or even plywood.

The surest way to stabilize a wing wall is to use a long 2×4 for the last wall stud, cut a hole through the subfloor to accommodate the extra length, and then attach the stud to a floor joist or other framing underneath the floor. This is effective particularly for walls that are in areas of heavy traffic or are designed to be covered with ceramic tile.

SOFFITS: Unless upper cabinets are custom-made, they do not extend to an 8-foot-high ceiling. Instead, there is a gap of about 1 foot above the upper cabinets because most people cannot reach higher. Occasionally, this gap is used to display items, such as bowls or baskets. More often, the space is filled by a soffit—a framed box covered with drywall and finished to match surrounding wall surfaces.

It is common practice to build soffits after the drywall is installed on the main walls and ceiling. The soffit frames are lifted into place and secured with nails or screws. Then the two outside surfaces are covered with drywall.

The finished depth of a soffit should be 13–14 inches. Upper cabinets are 12 inches deep, so the extra width accounts for any crooked walls or discrepancies in the cabinets themselves. This also permits decorative trim to be installed where the cabinet meets the bottom of the soffit.

STUD WALL CONSTRUCTION

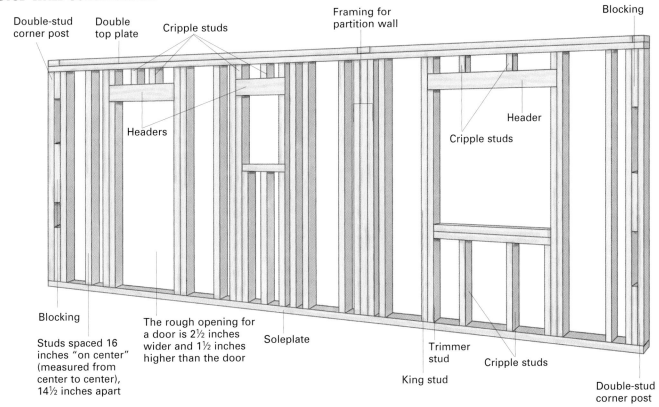

Double-stud corner post
Double top plate
Cripple studs
Framing for partition wall
Blocking
Headers
Header
Cripple studs
Blocking
Studs spaced 16 inches "on center" (measured from center to center), 14½ inches apart
The rough opening for a door is 2½ inches wider and 1½ inches higher than the door
Soleplate
Trimmer stud
Cripple studs
King stud
Double-stud corner post

ROUGHING-IN PLUMBING

Most kitchens include a sink, garbage disposer, and a dishwasher, but your remodeling plans may call for a second sink, an ice-making refrigerator, or a laundry area. In addition, a gas line may be needed for the range, cooktop, or oven. Installing new fixtures in the same locations as the previous ones can save time and money. If new fixtures are to be installed within a few inches of the old locations, you may be able to adjust plumbing or add flexible pipe extenders to account for the difference. If new fixtures are to be installed or old ones moved to new locations, new plumbing will have to be roughed-in.

Roughing-in plumbing means carefully measuring distances, estimating the slope of drainpipes, calculating pipe sizes, and installing pipe in open walls. Most of these measurements are governed by local building codes. For example, a kitchen sink with a dishwasher requires a 2-inch diameter drainpipe. If you are adding a washing machine to this drain line, you must increase the drainpipe diameter to 3 inches. Check local codes for plumbing requirements.

Gas lines and fittings are similar to water lines and plumbing fittings. However, moving gas appliances and installing new gas lines are jobs for a professional who is experienced with the work and who can test the lines after they are installed.

DRAIN AND VENT PIPES: Drains and vents work together as part of the whole plumbing system. If you are planning new sinks or appliances, you must consider where the drainpipes and vent stacks will be located and the sizes of the pipes that will be installed.

Drainpipes must slope at least ¼ inch for each foot of horizontal run. The locations of new drains are affected by your ability to create the proper slope between each drain and the main sewer line. The typical rough-in location for a sink drain stub—the place where the sink drain enters the wall—is 15 inches from the floor.

All plumbing fixtures must be vented to the roof through pipes or stacks. Codes usually specify a "trapping distance"—the maximum permissible distance between the sink trap and the vent stack. For a 1½-inch drainpipe, the distance is usually 3 feet; for a 2-inch drainpipe, the trapping distance typically is 5 feet.

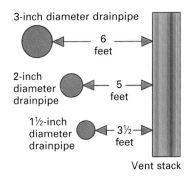

3-inch diameter drainpipe
6 feet
2-inch diameter drainpipe
5 feet
1½-inch diameter drainpipe
3½ feet
Vent stack

Drain traps set farther from a vent stack require larger diameter drainpipes. Sizes shown represent typical codes.

ROUGHING-IN THE SPACE
continued

Most codes prohibit changing direction of the vent stack from vertical to horizontal at any point lower than 42 inches above the floor. This restriction must be taken into account when a window is located directly above a sink. To solve the problem, a vertical vent stack can be located to one side of the window and accessed with a horizontal trap from the sink drain, as long as the trapping distance is within code guidelines.

WATER SUPPLY LINES: Run new water supply lines after the drainpipes and vent stacks have been installed. If your old system did not have shutoff valves for all fixtures, install them now. Shutoff valves allow you to turn off the water to an individual fixture in case repairs are needed. That way, you won't

PROTECT PIPES FROM FREEZING

To make sure pipes don't freeze during cold weather, take these precautions:
■ Locate all supply pipes within the insulated area of your home. Wrap heat tape and pipe insulation around vulnerable supply lines, such as pipes located in an unheated crawl space.
■ Keep a layer of blanket insulation between drainpipes and the home's exterior sheathing.
■ If you have installed flexible plastic pipe for supply lines, you should allow enough slack to account for 6 inches of expansion and contraction for every 50 feet of pipe.

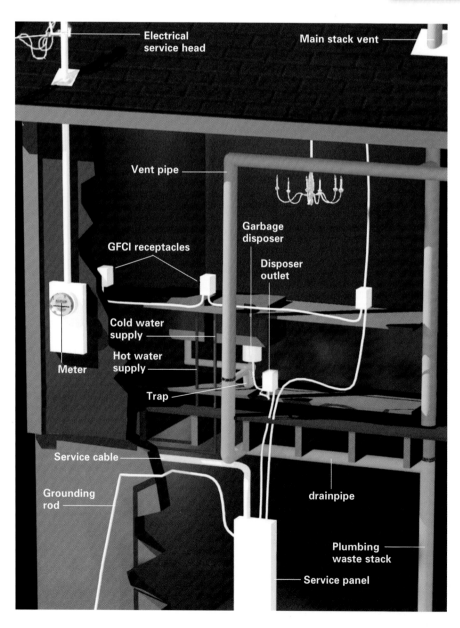

Electrical service head

Main stack vent

Vent pipe

Garbage disposer

GFCI receptacles

Disposer outlet

Cold water supply

Hot water supply

Meter

Trap

Service cable

Grounding rod

drainpipe

Plumbing waste stack

Service panel

have to shut off the water supply to the entire house. The typical rough-in location for the hot and cold water supply stubs is 19 inches from the floor.

A dishwasher will require a hot-water supply line typically made of flexible copper tubing that is $\frac{3}{8}$ inch in diameter. If the refrigerator has an ice maker, it will need a cold-water supply line. Check the manufacturer's recommendations to determine the size and location of this line.

ROUGHING-IN WIRING

New wiring includes installing electrical boxes for switches and receptacles in the open framing and running wire or cable to the boxes from the circuit breaker panel. Wiring from new lighting fixtures or appliances is joined to the wires from the panel at switches or junction boxes. If you plan to do electrical work yourself, first switch off the power at the service panel. Once wiring is roughed-in, it should be checked by a licensed electrician or a building inspector.

The first step is to plan the circuits. Depending on local codes, you may be able to extend existing circuits or you may have to install new circuits. If you are unsure, consult an electrician.

For safety, it's best to have new circuits installed that can handle additional loads adequately. Plan a separate circuit for each of these appliances:
- Electrical range (240-volt circuit)
- Electric cooktop (240-volt circuit)
- Gas cooktop (120-volt circuit for electronic controls and clock)
- Electric oven (240-volt circuit)
- Garbage disposer (120-volt circuit)
- Dishwasher (120-volt circuit)
- Built-in microwave (120-volt circuit)
- Trash compactor (120-volt circuit)
- Freezer (120-volt circuit)
- If you intend to include a planning center or workstation with a computer and printer, you should add a separate 120-volt circuit.

LOADING CIRCUITS: Codes do not specify how many receptacles to allow for each circuit, but it is common practice to allow no more than six. Receptacles over countertops should be placed no more than 4 feet apart, with at least one outlet over any single section of countertop longer than 12 inches. Locate over-the-counter receptacles 42 inches above the floor, normal receptacles 14 inches above the floor, and switch boxes 48 inches above the floor.

Lights should be installed on their own 120-volt circuit. Although it may be possible to wire new lights into an existing lighting circuit, it's a better idea to provide a separate circuit for any new fixtures.

Each new circuit requires its own circuit breaker at the service panel. Before installing new circuits, you'll need to see how much available space you have in the panel. Remember that circuits for 240-volt appliances require a double space.

If your present panel has little or no available space, you may have to install a subpanel. Check local codes to determine where a subpanel may be located, and how large (its amperage rating) it must be to handle the load you've planned.

If the present service is properly grounded, if it has a capacity of at least 100 amps, and if you are not adding any major appliances that require 240-volt circuits, your present service should be able to handle new kitchen circuits. Otherwise, you may need to upgrade your main service panel.

CABLE: For most installations, codes allow the use of nonmetallic sheathed cable, commonly called Romex™. Most codes require that cable be stapled every 4½ feet and within 8 inches of plastic boxes and within 12 inches of metal boxes. Many local codes do not allow wiring to be run horizontally through exterior wall studs. Instead, it must be run under the floor system and brought up through the soleplate for each outlet. Where wiring does run through walls, the holes in the studs cannot be drilled closer than 1½ inches from the edges of the studs.

When planning your wiring, don't forget to plan for additional telephones, stereo speakers, hard-wired smoke detectors, and security systems.

SIZING HEAVY-DUTY CIRCUITS

Appliance	Electrical Requirements	Wire Size	Receptacle
Electric water heater	240 volts, 20 to 40 amps	#12 for 20 amps or less, #10 for 30 amps	20-amp, 240-volt or 30-amp, 240-volt
Electric range	Typically 50 amps at 120/240 volts; check local code for plug and receptacle requirements.	Two #6 hot wires and a #8 neutral; for small units, two #8 hot and one #10 neutral	30-amp, 120/240-volt or 50-amp, 120/240-volt
Separate oven or cooktop	Connect both to a single 50 amp, 120/240-volt circuit or provide separate 30-amp circuits for each.	For a single circuit, see electric range, above; otherwise, 30-amp circuits take #10 wire.	
Microwave, refrigerator, dishwasher	Typically, 15 or 20 amps at 120 volts; however, each should have a separate circuit.	#12	15-amp, 120-volt

A design classic, the black-and-white floor is one of the most popular kitchen motifs. This one features 1-foot ceramic tile squares.

FLOORING

Many kinds of flooring are beautiful yet rugged enough for kitchen use. Most are relatively easy to install, although the job can take time.

If it's part of a large remodeling project, flooring usually is the last material to be installed. That way, the surface is protected from construction miscues, such as a dropped hammer or spilled paint. However, flooring should be installed before appliances—stove, refrigerator, or dishwasher—are put in place.

If your plans include ceramic or stone tiles, your floor system must be strong enough to carry the added weight. Have an architect or engineer calculate the strength of existing floor joists before proceeding. Subfloor materials should be no less than 1¼-inch thick so the floor remains stable. Any flexing of the subfloor likely will cause grout joints and tiles to crack.

Remember, if your design calls for continuous flooring between the kitchen and adjacent spaces, you'll want to select a product that looks and feels appropriate to all areas.

SILENCE THOSE SQUEAKS

Before you install new flooring, you should fix squeaking floors. Squeaks are common especially in older floors. Over time, subfloors and joists lose moisture and shrink, creating gaps that flex as you walk over them. When floor parts flex, they can rub against each other and against nails to produce annoying squeaks. Have one person walk over the floor and another mark locations that squeak. Then, stand near the squeaking area to apply weight and drive screws down through the flooring into joists to secure loose flooring. Because you'll be covering the screw heads with new flooring, you can drive the screws directly through the old flooring. Be sure screw heads are set below the surface of the old flooring, and fill any holes with putty before installing new flooring.

TYPES OF FLOORING

This well-planned vinyl flooring installation features few seams and works well in this monochromatic color scheme.

Vinyl flooring ranks among the most popular and least expensive options for kitchens. Durable and highly resistant to moisture, it requires little maintenance. Expect to pay from $1 per square foot (for vinyl tiles that you install yourself) to $15 per square foot (for high-quality sheet goods installed by a professional).

Vinyl comes in three grades:

■ **COMPOSITION** is the least expensive and is a mixture of vinyl and filler materials.

■ **ROTOVINYL** has a wear layer of clear vinyl over a photographic image imposed upon backing material. The thickness of the wear layer boosts durability and cost. Look for rotovinyl that is 10–25 millimeters thick.

■ **INLAID** vinyl's colors and patterns extend throughout the entire thickness of the material. Inlaid is the most expensive type of vinyl, but its pattern cannot be worn away.

All vinyls cut easily with shears or a utility knife and make good do-it-yourself materials.

Self-sticking vinyl tile beats all other floor coverings for ease of installation. However, the many seams created by the tiles are susceptible to moisture from kitchen spills. Eventually, the adhesive around the tiles may fail, causing the edges of the tile to separate from the subfloor.

Sheet goods are best for kitchens because there are few seams. Some sheet goods have a cushioned backing that makes them more comfortable for foot traffic.

Wood flooring comes in strips, parquet tiles, and wide planks. High-tech urethane and acrylic finishes and laminate construction make it nearly impervious to damage from moisture. As a result, more wood flooring is being installed in kitchens. For do-it-yourself installations, you may pay as little as $2 per square foot for wood parquet tiles. If a professional installs high-quality strip flooring, you'll pay about $7–12 per square foot.

Pre-finished hardwood laminate flooring locks together with tongue-and-groove edges. It is about ⅜ inch thick and usually is glued to the subfloor (some types are simply edge-glued together and installed over thin sheets of resilient foam rubber). All-wood strip hardwood flooring is usually ⅝ to ¾ inch thick and must be nailed to a subfloor that is at least ⅝ inch thick.

Ceramic tile, an extremely durable and beautiful kitchen flooring, comes in a wide variety of shapes, patterns, and textures. Ceramic tile can be installed over many existing surfaces, but you need to check the strength of your flooring system to ensure it can hold the added weight. This especially is true if you plan to cover existing ceramic tile with more tile. You'll probably need to remove the old tile—a messy and time-consuming job.

Tile costs as little as $4 per square foot for materials to $50 per square foot installed. Costs escalate for intricate patterns or unusually shaped tiles. For slate, granite, or limestone tiles, expect to pay $100 or more per square foot for materials and installation.

COVERING OLD FLOORING

Most flooring can be installed over existing flooring, with a few exceptions. Determine if the existing flooring is sound and in good repair. Loose flooring must be nailed down or reglued. Warped flooring should be nailed flat or leveled with a belt sander. Broken or missing flooring should be repaired or patched with filler and sanded flush with surrounding surfaces. Once repairs are made, be sure the existing flooring is free of all dirt, grease, and wax. Before covering any floor surface, check the guidelines below.

If your existing flooring is:

VINYL TILES OR SHEET GOODS: All new flooring can be installed over vinyl, with two exceptions. New sheet goods should not be installed over textured vinyl flooring. (Tiles made to simulate brick are a good example.) The texture is so pronounced that

Wood flooring adds style to even the simplest of kitchen designs.

sheet goods cannot be stapled to ceramic tile. Instead, use vinyl flooring adhesive. If you are installing new ceramic tile over old, check the strength of your flooring system to make sure it can take the added weight. Level the entire surface of the old ceramic tile floor with latex underlayment, then sand smooth.

CARPET: Old carpet must be removed completely.

CONCRETE SLABS: Consult with a professional remodeling contractor or concrete contractor to determine the condition of your slab and what provisions, if any, must be made before it can be covered with new flooring.

it will eventually show through new sheet goods. In this case, the old tiles must be removed. Also, do not install any vinyl over cushioned sheet goods. The cushioning may flex, breaking the adhesive bond with the new vinyl flooring. Wash old vinyl surfaces with a strong detergent to remove any wax.

WOOD FLOORING: You may install any type of flooring over wood, as long as the surface is completely flat. Fill any cracks or holes with wood filler and sand smooth. Nail down any loose flooring. Some wood floors feature V-grooves that must be filled with latex underlayment and sanded smooth before new flooring can be installed. If your new flooring requires a glued down installation, roughen the finish of old wood flooring with medium-grit sandpaper to remove the gloss and provide a better surface for adhesion.

CERAMIC TILE: Nail-down wood strip flooring cannot be installed over ceramic tile. You must remove the old tile. New vinyl

CAUTION!

Some older vinyl-type flooring materials contain asbestos. When sanded or cut, asbestos fibers become airborne. If inhaled, they can be a serious health hazard. If you suspect your flooring contains asbestos, you should contact your state department of environmental affairs or your local health department for information on how to proceed. If your remodeling plans call for removal of these materials, ask for advice about the proper methods of disposal.

Installing tough and beautiful ceramic tile is not a difficult project for the do-it-yourselfer.

REMOVING OLD FLOORING

Remove old flooring if it is damaged badly or is unsuitable as a base for new flooring (see *"Covering Old Flooring,"* page 48). Otherwise, cover your old flooring with a layer of plywood before installing new flooring.

Removing old flooring includes prying up baseboards and base shoe. Remember to take into account the height of your new floor. Layers of underlayment or flooring will reduce the height of appliance openings, especially undercounter dishwashers. Estimate the thickness of your new floor, then measure to make sure appliance openings will be large enough. You may have to shim up your countertop to gain space. This is a big job that requires you to unfasten the countertop from underneath, disconnect plumbing, and shim the countertop up with flat pieces of wood. To avoid this work, consider other options, such as smaller appliances or thinner flooring material.

If you plan to install new flooring without removing base cabinets, remember that the height of the toe kick—the space at the bottom of the cabinet—will be reduced.

TOOLS

Flat pry bar, hammer, hand saw.
For vinyl tiles: Heat gun.
For ceramic tiles: Cold chisel.

TOOL FACTS

Prying off old materials that have been glued to walls or floors takes patience and the correct tools. Small, flat pry bars about 12 inches long are good for starting the work because the fingers—the ends of the tool—are made of thin steel and are easy to force behind tiles and moldings. Never pry directly against drywall or flooring. Instead, insert thin pieces of wood to prevent damage to surrounding surfaces. It is helpful to use two prying tools in combination—one to hold open the gaps between old materials and surfaces and the other to do the actual prying.

Remove thresholds with a flat pry bar. If the threshold runs underneath a door stop or door jamb, you'll have to cut the jamb apart at its middle and remove the pieces.

Undercut door casings so new flooring can slide underneath. This is a much faster and neater solution than trying to cut the flooring to fit around the casing. Place a piece of the new flooring (and underlayment if you're using it) against the casing and mark the new floor height with a pencil. Saw the casing with a fine-tooth handsaw.

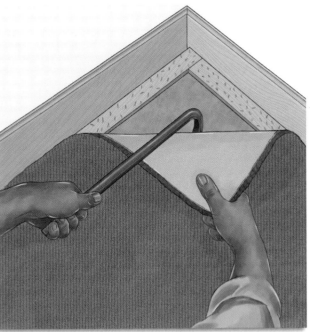

Remove vinyl cove base moldings by prying the molding away from the wall, using a 4-inch putty knife. Use the putty knife to scrape away any remaining adhesive. Old vinyl tiles can be warmed with a heat gun to soften the adhesive backing. Then remove the tiles with a 4-inch putty knife.

Carpet can be removed by loosening a corner and pulling it away from the tackless perimeter strips. Once the entire piece has been released, it can be rolled up and removed. Use a flat pry bar to remove the perimeter strips. Remove carpet pads by pulling up the pad and removing the carpet tacks with a flat pry bar.

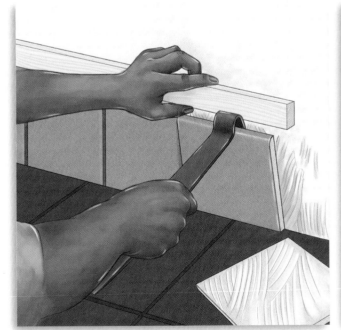

Remove ceramic base tiles one at a time with a flat pry bar. If possible, use the tool sideways so you apply pressure against the bottom plate of the stud wall. Otherwise, pry against a piece of 1×4 or similar scrap wood to prevent damaging the wall surface. Use a putty knife to scrape away any adhesive.

Old ceramic tiles must be broken apart with a hammer and the pieces pried up with a cold chisel. Wear eye protection and allow plenty of time for this job.

INSTALLING UNDERLAYMENT

The best way to ensure a smooth, flat, level surface for flooring installations is to cover your existing floor with plywood underlayment. Use high-quality, ¼-inch lauan plywood for underlayment. It is relatively lightweight, cuts easily, and is not difficult to install. It cannot be installed over ceramic tile or concrete (*refer to the guidelines on page 49*).

Plywood comes in 4×8-foot sheets at home-improvement centers and lumber stores. To determine how many sheets you require, multiply the length of your floor (in feet) by its width. This is the floor's square footage. Don't forget to include the square footage for any appliance alcoves, closets, or butler's pantry. To the total square footage, add 10 percent for waste. Divide this number by 32 (the area of a full sheet) to determine the number of plywood sheets you need.

For new installations of ceramic tile, you may want to install an underlayment of cementitious backer board. Backer board comes in 4×4-foot sheets that are ½-inch thick. It is fixed in place with 1-inch galvanized drywall screws. You can cut backer board by scoring the surface with a utility knife and snapping the pieces apart. Or, use a circular saw equipped with a masonry blade.

Backer board is a heavy material, but the methods of installation are similar to the instructions described here for plywood.

TOOLS

Hammer, tape measure, handsaw, putty knife, jigsaw, circular saw.
For cementitious backer board: Circular saw with masonry-cutting blade, utility knife, electric drill with power screw tips.

TOOL FACTS

The masonry-cutting blade used to cut backer board is readily available in hardware stores and home-improvement centers. It is a flat disk of abrasive material that grinds away brick, stone, or tile, leaving a fairly smooth edge. When cutting hard masonry materials, keep a firm grip on the circular saw and proceed slowly. For thick materials, such as ½-inch backer board, take two passes, setting the blade to cut only halfway through on the first pass, finishing the cut on the second pass.

1 Remove appliances, such as refrigerator, stove, and dishwasher. Use pieces of new flooring and underlayment when measuring to determine if the new floor height will permit appliances to be replaced. If not, you may have to shim up countertops or remove old flooring to gain the space needed to replace appliances.

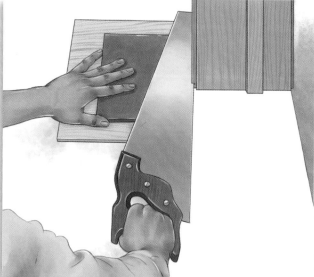

2 Remove all base moldings. Using pieces of new flooring and underlayment as a guide, mark and undercut door casings to accommodate new floor height. Cut casings with a fine-tooth handsaw.

3 Begin installation of the underlayment against the longest wall or run of base cabinets. Use a circular saw or jigsaw to cut the underlayment to fit. For long straight cuts, use a straightedge to guide the saw.

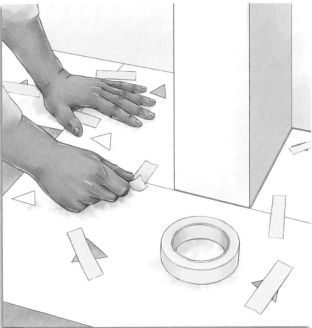

4 Make a template of cardboard or paper for irregular areas. Transfer the shape of the template to the plywood for cutting.

5 Nail the underlayment with 6d ringshank nails driven every 6 inches along the edges of the plywood and spaced every 8 inches throughout the sheet. Set the nail heads just below the surface of the plywood. Leave ⅛ inch between panels for expansion.

6 Cover all remaining areas, staggering the seams. Fill small areas, such as appliance alcoves, last. Use a putty knife to cover nail heads, depressions, holes, and gaps with latex underlayment. Let the filler dry, then sand it flush with the surrounding surfaces.

INSTALLING WOOD OR VINYL FLOOR TILES

Installing vinyl or wood parquet tiles is a relatively easy do-it-yourself project. Vinyl tiles are available with adhesive backing that makes them simple to install. Some vinyl tiles and wood tiles must be set in flooring adhesive.

Careful layout is the key to a successful project. Once layout lines have been established, dry fit rows of tiles in all directions to make sure the finished design will be attractive. This is especially important if the tiles will extend into adjacent areas such as hallways. In a hallway, an asymmetrical layout, such as a row of full tiles running along one wall and a row of narrow, partial tiles along the opposite wall, may look awkward and poorly planned.

Begin tile installation at the center of the room and work toward the walls. Be sure that the underlayment is completely clean—dirt and dust can prevent the tiles from sticking completely. Where tiles meet walls, base cabinets, or other vertical surfaces, leave a ¼-inch gap for expansion. The gap will be hidden by base moldings.

Measure and cut partial vinyl tiles using metal shears or a utility knife. Cut wood parquet tiles with a jigsaw. Turn wood tiles upside down for cutting to prevent the blade from chipping the top surfaces of the tiles. Carefully transpose measurements to an upside-down tile so that it will fit the layout correctly. For complex cuts, it's a good idea to make a cardboard template in the shape of the space you need to fit and use the template to mark the tile for cutting.

TOOLS

Tape measure, framing square, utility knife or metal shears, jigsaw, chalk reel and line, putty knife, notched trowel.

1 *Establish a primary layout line by measuring from opposite walls or base cabinets to determine the center of the floor area. Snap a chalk line that bisects the room. This is the primary layout line.*

2 *Measure and mark the center of the primary line. From this center point, use a framing square and draw a second line perpendicular to the first. Use the edge of the framing square to extend this secondary line a distance of at least 3 feet. You'll use a geometric exercise called a "carpenter's triangle" in Step 3 to make sure the lines are perpendicular.*

3 *From the intersection of the two lines, measure and mark the primary chalk line at a distance of 4 feet. Measure and mark the secondary line at a distance of 3 feet from the intersection. If the lines are perpendicular, the distance between the marks will be 5 feet.*
If necessary, make adjustments to the secondary line. When you are satisfied with the results, extend the secondary line across the room by snapping a chalk line.

4 *Dry fit tiles along the layout lines in all directions. Check to make sure the layout is satisfactory. If necessary, adjust the layout by snapping a new chalk line parallel to the original.*

5 *Begin installing tiles at the intersection of the layout lines. Apply the tiles to one section of the floor at a time, using the sequence indicated in the illustration. When installing tiles over flooring adhesive, work small areas at a time. Spread only enough adhesive to allow you to place four or five tiles.*

HINTS FOR TILE INSTALLATION

Self-sticking tiles are easy to install but adhere instantly to the subfloor, leaving little room for error. Misaligned tiles can be removed by gently warming them with a heat gun or household iron.

Make paper or cardboard templates of corners or unusually shaped obstacles. Trace the outline of the template on the tile and cut it to shape before removing the backing and exposing the adhesive. When working with wood tiles, you'll want to trace onto the backs so that the tile can be cut upside down. Pay attention to how you place the template on an upside-down tile—the template must also be turned upside down.

Use a notched trowel to spread flooring adhesive. Usually these tools have notches of varying sizes on each edge of the blade. The adhesive manufacturer's instructions should indicate the appropriate notches to use with your installation.

When kneeling on newly installed tiles, use a piece of scrap plywood to distribute your weight and prevent the tiles from shifting.

Store a few extra tiles in a cool, dry place. You can use them if your floor ever needs to be repaired.

INSTALLING GLUE-DOWN WOOD STRIP FLOORING

Many kinds of prefinished hardwood flooring are manufactured for easy installation. They are often made as planks—pieces that look like two or three hardwood strips glued together. Planks usually come in 4- or 6-inch widths that can be installed much faster than individual 2-inch strips.

These types of flooring are made to be glued to the subfloor. Most are $5/16$ or $3/8$ inch thick so they are lightweight and cut easily with a jigsaw or handsaw.

Laminate construction features a thin top layer of hardwood bonded to plywood. It makes glue-down hardwood very stable despite shifts in temperature and humidity. Tough polyurethane coatings help protect against moisture.

FLOATING ON FOAM: Some types of pre-finished flooring are not glued directly to the floor but are "floated" on a thin layer of foam rubber. Edge-gluing the pieces together gives them stability. Floating floor systems can be installed over a variety of existing surfaces, including ceramic tile, textured vinyl, and concrete. Always check the manufacturer's recommendations before proceeding.

WHICH WAY TO GO: Hardwood flooring customarily is installed parallel to the longest wall of the room and parallel to hallway walls. Check to make sure your installation will conform to these guidelines. It is possible to change direction of the flooring, but these changes should be established at doorways. When changing directions of hardwood flooring, plan to take advantage of the flooring's tongue-and-groove ends so that all joints are tight.

TOOLS FOR GLUE-DOWN INSTALLATION

Measuring tape, chalk reel and line, mallet, notched trowel, jigsaw, rented flooring roller.

TOOLS FOR FLOATING PLANK FLOOR

Measuring tape, mallet, jigsaw.

INSTALLING A FLOATING PLANK FLOOR

1 Unroll the foam backing and cut it to fit the shape of the kitchen floor. Use masking tape to keep seams together. Begin installation along the longest wall or run of base cabinets. Install the first row with the tongue side out (away from the wall). Leave a ½-inch gap at the wall for expansion, using blocks of wood for spacers. That way, you can apply pressure to subsequent rows in order to seat the tongues firmly inside the grooves.

2 Use carpenter's glue to join the planks together. Apply the glue to all tongues, then set each plank into place. Use a mallet and a piece of scrap flooring to tap boards into position and create tight joints. Wipe up any excess glue.

INSTALLING GLUE-DOWN WOOD STRIP FLOORING

1 *Measure 30 inches out from the longest wall or base cabinet run and snap a chalk line parallel to the wall. To begin, you will install a first row of flooring at the line and work away from the wall. The 30-inch space is for kneeling in while you begin installation. You'll finish this space after the larger portion of flooring is complete.*

2 *Apply adhesive according to the manufacturer's instructions. Apply only enough to work a few rows at a time. Place the first row of flooring along the layout line with the grooved side away from your 30-inch work space. Apply carpenter's glue to the tongue-and-groove ends of each piece just before installing. Don't glue the long edges. Wipe up excess glue immediately.*

3 *Use a straightedge or string line to check that the first row is set straight. Insert the tongue of the next piece into the groove of the preceding row and lower the piece onto the adhesive bed. Slide the tongue-and-groove ends together. Use a mallet to tap boards into position and create tight joints. Use a protective piece of scrap between the mallet and the flooring.*

4 *Leave a ½-inch expansion space at walls. This space will be covered by baseboard moldings. Use templates of cardboard or paper to trace irregular shapes and transfer them to boards. Use a jigsaw to cut the flooring. Use a heavy floor roller to bond the flooring to the subfloor. You can rent floor rollers from rental outlets and flooring distributors.*

INSTALLING SHEET VINYL

Sheet vinyl is manufactured in 6- and 12-foot widths. Measure your kitchen carefully to determine if your sheet goods can be installed without seams. If seams are necessary, plan the installation so the seams occur in inconspicuous or low-traffic areas. If your vinyl flooring will extend into adjacent areas, such as hallways, plan to put seams at passage doorways.

The challenge of installing sheet goods is to cut the vinyl correctly so it matches the outline of your kitchen floor. There's no second chance to do the job right (unless you buy more material). The best way to prevent errors is to make a paper template of the floor area. Make a template using heavy paper—a roll of butcher's paper works well for this purpose. Some flooring manufacturers have kits that include everything you'll need for creating a template.

Next, you'll need a clean, dry area large enough to allow you to trace the template onto the vinyl flooring. A garage or basement floor may serve this purpose, but first it must be thoroughly cleaned. Dirt or tiny stones that

stick to the bottom of the vinyl during cutting will get trapped under the sheet when it is installed. Over time, these imperfections may show through or even pierce the surface.

Sheet vinyl is installed using either perimeter staples or glue. Glue-down vinyls can be installed over any flat and level surface. Stapled installations require a wood substrate to hold the staples.

Remember that you'll first need to remove any base moldings and undercut door casings by the thickness of a handsaw blade—about ⅛ inch—so that the vinyl will slip under the casings.

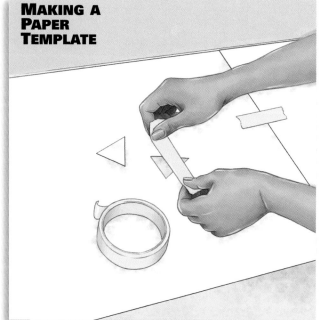

MAKING A PAPER TEMPLATE

1 Use heavy 12- or 18-inch wide paper, such as butcher's paper. Position the edges of the paper against the walls, leaving about a ⅛-inch gap. Use a utility knife to cut holes in the paper about every 18 inches, alternating from the front edge of the paper and the back. Place pieces of masking tape over the holes to prevent the paper from shifting.

2 Place paper around the room, cutting the paper to fit against corners. Overlap seams about 2 inches and tape together. Slide paper under door casings.

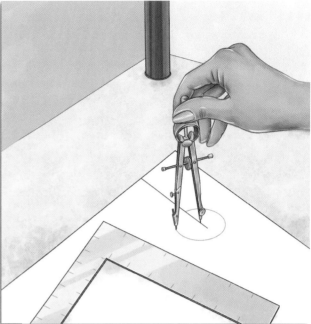

3 To account for obstructions, such as pipes, you'll need to trace the outline of the obstruction onto the template. Start by measuring from the wall to the edge of the obstruction. For pipes and other round objects, measure to the center.

4 Transfer the measurement to a separate piece of paper. Trace the outline of the object on the paper. For round objects, use a compass to create a circle from the centerpoint measurement.

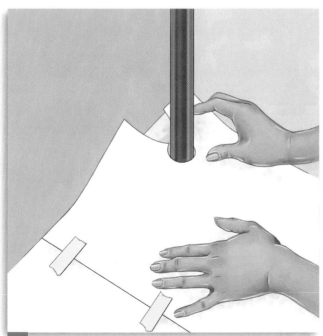

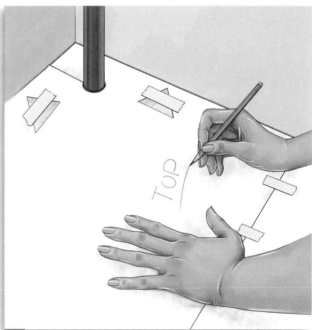

5 Cut out the template, then cut a slit from the cutout to the edge of the paper. Fit the paper around the obstruction and check for accuracy. When you're satisfied, tape the paper into place and attach it to adjoining sheets.

6 When the template is completed, indicate the top side with a mark. Then gently roll or loosely fold it and carry it to the area where you'll be cutting the vinyl.

INSTALLING SHEET VINYL
continued

INSTALLING VINYL SHEET GOODS

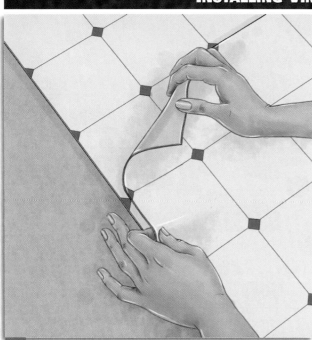

1 Unroll the sheet vinyl on a clean, dry, flat surface. Make sure it is pattern-side up. If your installation requires more than one piece of vinyl, plan the seams carefully. Overlap the pieces at least 2 inches. Position the sheets so that the patterns match, then tape the pieces together using duct tape.

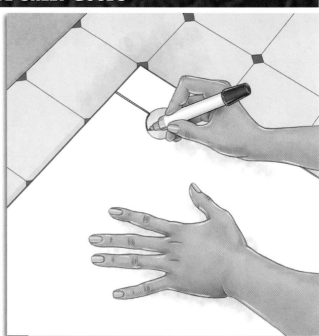

2 Align the template on top of the sheet goods. Make sure any seams are located in areas you planned. Tape the template to the vinyl. Trace the outline of the template onto the sheets with a fine-point marking pen.

3 After the tracing is complete, remove the template. Cut along the tracing lines with a utility knife. If possible, avoid standing or kneeling on the sheet goods.

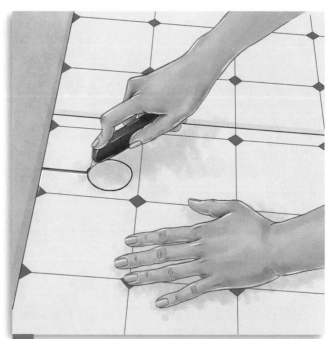

4 Cut holes for pipes or other obstructions according to the template outline. Then cut an access slit from the hole to the nearest edge of the sheet goods. If possible, follow the decorative pattern of the sheet so that the knife cuts will be hidden.

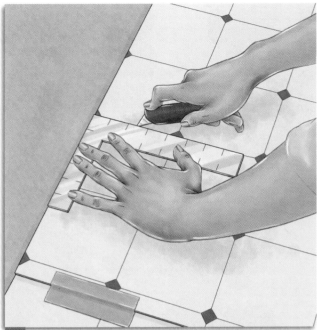

5 *Roll up the flooring, carry it to the kitchen, and unroll it. Sheets are awkward to handle, so recruit some help to avoid damage when you carry and unroll large pieces. Position the sheets carefully. At seams, trim the excess by cutting through both overlapped edges. Use a straightedge, such as a framing square, as a guide.*

6 *If possible, follow the decorative pattern of the vinyl sheet so that the knife cut won't be noticeable. After cutting the seam, you'll be left with two pieces of scrap. Remove the scrap; the two sheets should be pattern-matched.*

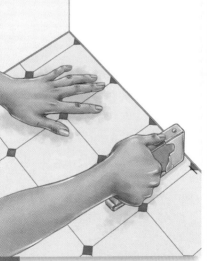

7 *To affix the vinyl to the subfloor, begin at the seams. Gently fold back the edges about 1 foot and use a notched trowel or putty knife to apply a 4-inch-wide swath of flooring adhesive to the subfloor. Place the seam edges into the adhesive one at a time, making sure the seam is tight. Use a hard rubber roller or rolling pin to help bond the flooring to the subfloor.*

8 *Use ⅜-inch staples to fasten the edges to wooden subfloors. Drive the staples every 4 inches, about ½ inch from walls or base cabinet kick plates. At obstructions, gently fold back the vinyl to expose the subfloor. Encircle obstructions with a 4-inch-wide band of flooring adhesive. Then replace the vinyl and bond it to the subfloor with a hard rubber roller.*

SUCCESS TIPS FOR BEAUTIFUL INSTALLATIONS

Ceramic tile or concrete subfloors require a 4-inch band of adhesive around the perimeter of the kitchen. Work small sections at a time, and bond the vinyl to the subfloor with a hard rubber roller or rolling pin.

Certain types of vinyl sheet goods require adhesive to be applied under the entire sheet. To do so, you'll need to position the sheet and cut any seams (Steps 7 and 8). Then gently fold back about half the sheet and apply flooring adhesive according to the manufacturer's recommendations. Replace the sheet and repeat the procedure for the other portion of the sheet goods. Bond the vinyl to the subfloor with a hard rubber roller or rolling pin.

INSTALLING CERAMIC TILE

Elegant and extremely durable, ceramic tile can be glued to most clean, level, well-bonded surfaces. Installed properly, it is impervious to water and will last for decades with little maintenance.

Ceramic tile should be installed over subfloors no less than 1¼ inches in total thickness. Thinner subfloors may flex, causing the tiles to break or grout to crack. If your subflooring needs to be strengthened, add exterior grade plywood or cementitious backer board (see "Using Backer Board," below).

RAISING HEIGHT AND WEIGHT: If you plan to install new tile directly over existing tile surfaces, you should have an experienced remodeling contractor or architect check your floor system. You may have to strengthen your floor joists to support the added weight.

Adding layers of tile and subflooring will raise the height of your finished floor. Before installing tile, measure to make sure doors and appliance openings will accommodate the increased height. If necessary, trim the bottoms of doors or shim up countertops.

CAUTION, CURVES AHEAD: Floor tile is thicker than wall tile and more difficult to cut. Straight cuts can be made with a tile cutter, but curves are challenging.

Professionals often use small routers with diamond-tipped blades to make intricate curved cuts in ceramic tile. If precision is important to the appearance of your job, you may want to contact a professional about cutting complex shapes for you.

Use cardboard templates to transfer the shapes to tiles for cutting, and then take the marked tiles to your professional. You may spend more time and more money this way, but the results can reward that investment.

As with any tile, careful layout is the key to success. Make layout lines as shown on pages 54–55, and dry fit tiles before beginning the installation process.

TOOLS

Notched trowel, rubber mallet, tile cutter, tile sander, vise, tile saw, grout float, grout sponge.

USING BACKER BOARD

Cementitious backer board is available in 4×4-foot sheets, ½-inch thick. It is heavy and more expensive than plywood, but it is made specifically for tile installations. Cut backer board by scoring it with a utility knife and snapping it along the score line. Or, it can be cut with a circular saw equipped with a masonry-cutting blade. When installing backer board, leave ⅛-inch gaps between sheets and ¼-inch gaps along walls and other vertical surfaces.

Use an electric drill and power screw tips to fix backer board to the subfloor with galvanized 1-inch drywall screws. Drive screws every 6 inches along the edge of the material and every 8 inches throughout the field. It's a good idea to predrill screw holes at the edges of the backer board to prevent crumbling the material. Set the heads of the screws flush with the surface. Seams between sheets should be covered with fiberglass mesh tape imbedded in latex underlayment compound or similar leveling compound. Take care to "feather out" the edges of the compound so that the surface is as flat as possible. Let the compound dry completely and sand out any bumps or ridges.

1 *Start at the center point of your layout lines. Use a notched trowel to apply adhesive according to the manufacturer's directions. Take care not to cover the layout lines with adhesive. Set the tiles in the sequence as shown. Work one quadrant of the layout at a time, spreading just enough adhesive to set five or six tiles. Plastic spacers maintain grout lines between the tiles. At walls and other vertical surfaces, leave a ¼-inch gap.*

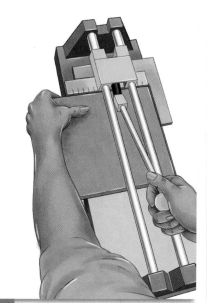

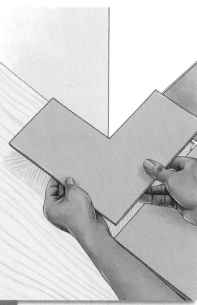

2 Use a rubber mallet to set the tiles into the adhesive bed. Or, use a piece of scrap lumber covered in carpet and gently tap the lumber with a hammer.

3 Make straight cuts with a tile cutter. Place the tile face-up in the cutter and adjust the width. Score by pulling the cutting wheel firmly. Snap the tile and smooth rough edges with a tile sander.

4 For corners and other irregular shapes, make a cardboard template to fit. Transfer the shape of the template to a tile and mark the tile for cutting.

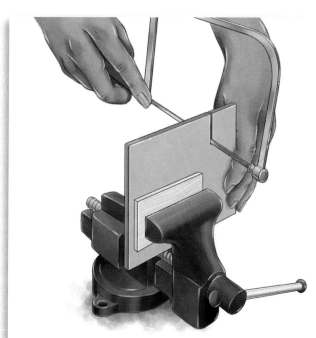

5 Cut irregular shapes by securing the tile in a vise. Use pieces of scrap wood between the jaws of the vise and the tile to prevent scratching the tile surface. Cut with a tile saw. Cutting tiles by hand can be a long process. If you have many to cut, consider renting an electric tile saw, sometimes called a wet saw, or taking marked tiles to a professional tile installer for cutting.

6 After the tiles are set, allow the adhesive to cure overnight. Then apply grout according to the manufacturer's directions. Hold the grout float at about a 60-degree angle and use a sweeping motion to force the grout into joints. Clean up excess with a damp grout sponge (a grout sponge has rounded edges that prevent scraping the grout out of the joints). Rinse the sponge often. Let grout cure about 15 minutes, then wipe off any haze with a soft, dry rag. Allow grout to cure for five to seven days, then apply silicone sealer to the entire floor.

These cabinets were designed specifically for this kitchen. The homeowners saved money by doing the installation work themselves.

CABINETS

Cabinets influence the look and function of a kitchen more than any other item. They also influence your budget—as much as 60 percent of the price of a kitchen remodeling project may be spent on new cabinets.

To save money, consider salvaging your existing cabinets. If they are of sound construction and in good working order, you can repaint them with tough, water-resistant enamel or reface them with real wood veneer to give your kitchen a facelift.

If you decide to replace your old cabinets, you can save money by doing the installation yourself. Many manufacturers produce cabinets in standard, modular sizes that make planning and installation relatively easy. You also may purchase unfinished cabinets and paint or stain them to match your design.

STRATEGIES FOR REVIVING OLD CABINETS

■ Repair scratches and nicks to provide a good surface for painting or refacing. To complete the facelift, replace cabinet hardware—hinges, drawer pulls, and door knobs. Make sure to select hardware that matches existing holes. Otherwise, you'll have to fill the old holes.

■ Repair any doors that have open joints, which result from failure of the glue that holds the parts together. Doors should be removed and reglued. Remove the damaged door and see whether the joint can be drawn together with a clamp. If so, remove the clamp and gently force the joint apart until there is room enough to apply carpenter's glue. Reclamp the door and wipe up any excess glue. Allow to dry overnight. If the joint cannot be drawn together with clamping pressure, check to see if it is blocked by dirt or grit that can be removed.

■ Add interesting details to door fronts by applying decorative wood moldings. This strategy works best on flat doors, sometimes called flush doors.

Many molding styles are available at lumber stores and home-improvement centers, so you should be able to find one that fits your kitchen design. Cut the moldings with mitered corners and apply in rectangular patterns to doors and drawers. Attach moldings with brad finish nails and carpenter's glue. Fill nail holes with filler and sand flush.

■ Replace doors and drawer fronts if they are badly worn but the cabinet bodies and face frames are sound. This strategy allows you to improve the look of your cabinets without incurring the considerable expense of a full replacement. Door and drawer front replacement works especially well with painted cabinets. Matching the color of stained cabinets can be more difficult. When replacing doors and drawer fronts, measure each one carefully so that replacements fit precisely. Most home-improvement centers carry a variety of pre-fabricated cabinet door and drawer fronts.

REVITALIZING CABINETS WITH PAINT

You can renew your kitchen easily and inexpensively by painting the cabinets. You'll get good results if you take time to prepare surfaces carefully and use top-quality paints and brushes. When painting, always provide good lighting. A portable work light can move with you as you paint each cabinet. For a completely fresh look, paint the insides of your cabinets as well.

Cabinets endure years of use and are washed frequently. For that reason, they should be painted with at least two coats of heavy-duty gloss or semi-gloss enamel. Prepare all surfaces with careful sanding, cleaning, and priming to make sure the paint will adhere well. Use synthetic bristle brushes for latex paints and natural bristle brushes for alkyd paints.

Stained and varnished cabinets can be painted, but first roughen the surfaces with fine sandpaper to remove any gloss and provide a good base for the primer. Alkyd paints work best when covering varnished surfaces. Always provide adequate ventilation when working with paints, especially alkyd paints that produce strong odors and take several hours to dry.

Removing doors and drawers and painting them in another location, such as a garage, is always a good idea. Set drawers on end and place cabinet doors on small blocks so that all edges are accessible.

TOOLS

Electric palm sander, screwdriver, paint scraper, paint brushes, paint roller.

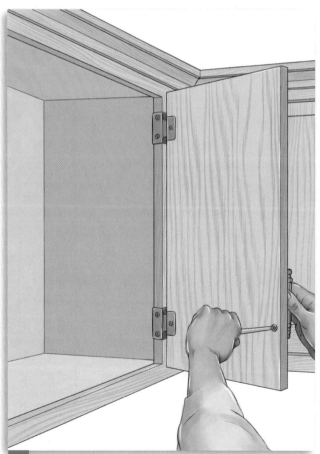

1 Empty cabinets. Remove cabinet doors and drawers. If you plan to reuse your existing hardware, unscrew all hinges, pulls, knobs, and closers and set them aside, keeping all screws and bolts.

2 Wash all cabinet surfaces with a mild solution of trisodium phosphate, available at hardware stores. Let the surface dry thoroughly. Use a paint scraper to remove any loose or peeling paint. Sand surfaces with 120-grit (medium) sandpaper. Clean off dust completely.

3 *Start painting cabinets at the least accessible area. If you are painting the inside of your cabinets, begin with the interior of corner cabinets. Always begin at the uppermost portion of the cabinets and work down. Paint large surface areas, such as the exposed ends of cabinets, with a short-nap roller.*

4 *Lay doors flat for painting, but use small blocks or other suitable spacers to keep the doors from touching floors or work surfaces. Paint recessed panels first, working toward the outside edges of the door. Check often for drips at the bottom edges of your work.*

5 *Set drawers on their back ends for painting. Let the paint dry thoroughly before reinstalling hardware. Drying times will vary, depending on the type of paint used, the texture of the surface, and the room's heat and humidity (always longer than you would prefer).*

FAUX FINISHED

To give your cabinets a customized look, try a faux finish. The example shown here is a multistep process using two shades of oil-based green paint. The lighter color is applied first and allowed to dry. The darker color is applied and immediately blotted with plastic wrap to produce a mottled effect. Because oil-based paints are slow-drying, the painter has plenty of time to work with the second coat.

RESURFACING CABINETS

Resurfacing puts a bright new face on your cabinets. The process involves covering cabinet frames and ends with adhesive wood veneers, then installing new doors and drawer fronts with matching wood grain. With resurfacing, there's no need to tear out sturdy old cabinets. The process costs about half as much as a complete cabinet replacement.

Before you begin, carefully research the availability of materials. Many home-improvement centers supply replacement doors and drawer fronts, but usually these items are available in stock sizes and cannot be custom-fitted. Also, wood varieties may be limited. You'll need to take a complete inventory of your doors and drawer fronts and purchase replacements that are exactly the same sizes. Buy veneer that matches the wood species of your doors and drawers to give stained finishes a uniform appearance.

Applying the veneer is not difficult, but it requires careful measurements and precise cutting with a utility knife. Remember that pieces cut too small will be wasted, but too-large pieces can be trimmed to fit even after they are installed. For the best adhesion, the cabinet surfaces must be completely clean and free of dust. Before applying veneers, wipe all surfaces with a tack rag.

Some companies make resurfacing kits that include all necessary materials. You'll need to provide accurate measurements of your kitchen cabinets and all doors and drawer fronts. Kit manufacturers offer a variety of styles and finishes. Locate a refinishing kit manufacturer by inquiring at local kitchen design service providers.

TOOLS
Screwdriver, paint scraper, utility knife, straightedge, hard rubber roller.

TOOL FACTS
A tack rag is invaluable for removing dust from work surfaces. You can buy tack rags at hardware stores or make them yourself. Use a square piece of cheesecloth about 24 inches wide. Moisten the cloth with water, then add several teaspoons of turpentine. Squeeze out excess moisture, then add several drops of varnish. Store tack rags in an airtight jar.

1 *Remove cabinet doors and drawers. Clean surfaces with a hardware-store solution of trisodium phosphate. After drying, scrape loose or peeling paint. Fill blemishes with latex filler, let dry, and sand filler flush. Sand cabinets lightly. Wipe away dust with a tack rag.*

2 *Apply the veneer to cabinet ends first, then cover the vertical face frame members, or stiles. Horizontal members, called rails, are covered last. Use a utility knife and a straightedge to cut the veneers. Make all cuts on a smooth wooden surface to prevent dulling the blade.*

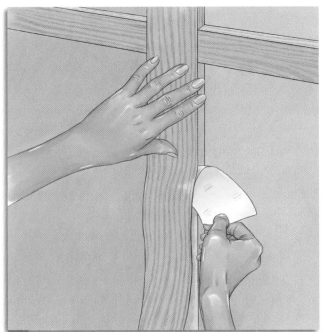

3 Dry fit cut veneer pieces before applying. Peel the backing off one corner of the veneer, align it, and press the exposed corner to adhere the piece. Peel off the remainder of the backing, pressing the veneer to the cabinet surface as you go. Trim excess with a utility knife. When all stiles have been covered, apply veneer to the rails. Use a hard rubber roller to adhere the veneer.

4 Stain all doors, drawer fronts, and unfinished veneers. Apply two coats of clear polyurethane to seal the finish against moisture. Apply cabinet hardware and remount all doors and drawers.

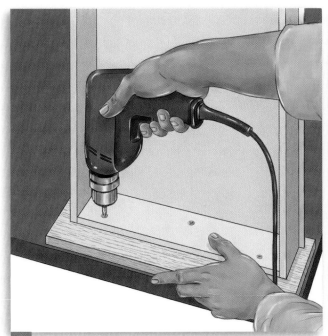

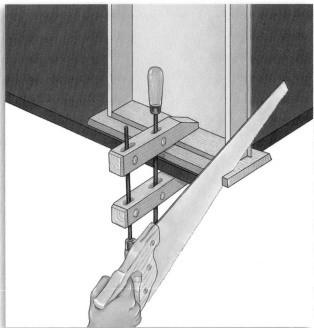

5 Drawer fronts are made from a single piece of wood or have a decorative face panel attached to the front of the drawer box. Old decorative face panels can be removed by unscrewing the fasteners that hold them in place. The screw heads are accessible inside the drawer.

6 One-piece fronts must be modified. Attaching a new front will lengthen the drawer slightly, so first check that the drawer glides and cabinet allow room. Then, use a handsaw to remove all overhanging edges from the old drawer front. Attach new face panels by drilling shallow pilot holes and driving screws from inside the drawer.

SELECTING NEW CABINETS

This kitchen makes good use of a hallway leading to a breakfast nook with a narrow pantry cabinet designed to match the style of the kitchen cabinets. This customized unit features plenty of low-cost open shelving, including a place for spices at one end.

Select cabinets thoughtfully. Shoppers face a bewildering array of styles and materials. Quality and price comparisons will lead you through custom cabinet dealers, kitchen retail stores, and home-improvement centers. But it's worth your time to research the possibilities and make an informed decision. Installing cabinets yourself is time-consuming and requires moderate do-it-yourself skills. If you have the expertise and the time, you may be able to reduce expenses or trade your labor for an upgrade in cabinet quality.

BASIC TYPES OF CABINETRY

■ **PREASSEMBLED STOCK CABINETS** offer consistent quality and ready availability at home-improvement centers. They are usually the most affordable type of cabinetry. Stock cabinets are made and finished on an assembly line, packed in boxes, and stored in warehouses. If an item is missing at your local supplier, usually it can be ordered and delivered within a few days. Standardized dimensions and modular designs of stock cabinets greatly simplify the job of tailoring cabinets to fit your kitchen. You can order a run of cabinets that comes within an inch or two of fitting, then make up the difference with fillers between the cabinets. Specialized units, such as lazy-Susans and open shelving, also are available as stock items. Many home-improvement centers also offer free design services if you purchase cabinets from them. An experienced designer can help you select and order cabinets that meet your needs.
■ **SEMICUSTOM CABINETS** are factory-made to your specifications. You choose the materials, finishes, colors, door and hardware styles, and cabinet sizes and configurations from selections the manufacturer makes available. Although your choices are somewhat limited, you can create variety by combining features and styles. Semicustom cabinet runs are tailored precisely to your kitchen space and may take four to 12 weeks for delivery.
■ **CUSTOM CABINETS** are tailored specifically to fit your kitchen and to incorporate any specialized ideas for storage or configurations. Custom cabinets offer advantages of special

sizes, unusual door designs, and virtually custom types of finishes. For example, you can specify extra height for base cabinets if you are tall or special colors to match fabrics or flooring. These types of cabinets are the most expensive and require the most lead time to build and deliver. They usually are available from local cabinetmakers who will take all necessary measurements and are readily available to discuss any special needs you might have.

CHECKING CABINETS FOR QUALITY

A good indicator of overall quality is drawer construction. If you pull a drawer out about ½ inch and let it go, it should close by itself. Self-closing drawers are mounted on a pair of quality metal slides with ball-bearing rollers. These are stronger and smoother than nylon slides or roller mechanisms installed beneath the drawers. Quality metal slides are rated to support 75 pounds or more per pair. There should be a stop that prevents the drawer from sliding all the way out.

Remove the drawer and check to see how it has been assembled. Quality drawers feature sides fastened to backs and fronts with interlocking dovetail joints or with dowels and screws. Lesser-quality drawers use staples and glue.

Examine the drawer bottoms. The bottom material should be at least as thick as the sides—about ⅜ inch. Anything less and the bottom may sag under heavy loads, such as

There's not much wasted space in this kitchen—even the toe kicks have been utilized for storage with slide-out drawers for canned goods, paper products, even a stepladder.

trays of silverware. Bottom panels should be fitted into grooves in the drawer sides.

Top-of-the-line wood cabinets have solid doors with grain that matches any exposed frame. Any exposed sides, backs, or shelves should be made of solid wood or plywood. Hidden backs, shelves, and drawer parts can be made of high-quality particleboard—it's a good choice for humid locations, such as kitchens—especially when it is covered with plastic or wood veneer. For less expense, you'll find doors and door frames made of plywood, veneered particleboard, or wood-grain laminates.

CABINET FINISHES

Cabinets can be purchased finished or unfinished. Unfinished cabinets can be finished by a do-it-yourselfer, but the process requires a large, well-ventilated, dust-free environment.

An appliance garage is just one of the many items available from makers of stock cabinets. The sliding tambour door keeps small appliances out of sight when not in use.

CABINET COSTS PER RUNNING FOOT

Type of Cabinet	Average Stock Cabinets	Semi Custom	Custom
Laminate Cabinet	$70–190	$130–225	$270–360
Veneer Cabinet	$90–190	N/A	N/A
Solid Wood Cabinet	$180–270	$200–360	$360–420
Painted Wood Cabinet	$200–360	$225–270	$300–400

Today's cabinet finishes are tough and durable. Most feature an undercoat of paint, stain, or custom glazing, covered by layers of clear topcoats that require little maintenance. In general, less expensive cabinets provide fewer topcoat layers than pricier cabinets.

For residential use, topcoats include lacquer, catalyzed varnishes, and urethanes. Lacquer is a good finish that's relatively easy to repair, although it is not as resistant to household solvents as catalyzed varnishes and urethanes. Fine, custom-made cabinetry often features many layers of clear lacquer that is hand-rubbed between applications to provide a deep, lustrous shine. Lacquer can be applied by the do-it-yourselfer, but results are best using a spray applicator.

Catalyzed varnishes provide tough, clear finishes with more durability than lacquer. Manufacturers prefer these finishes because they can be "force-dried," which greatly

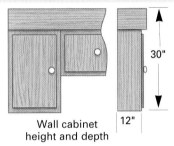

Wall cabinet height and depth | 30" | 12"

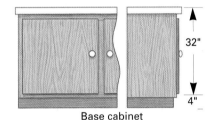

Base cabinet | 32" | 4"

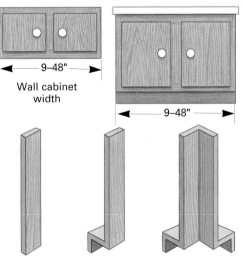

Wall cabinet width | 9–48"

9–48"

Wall filler strip   Base filler strip   Corner filler strip

MEASUREMENTS FOR STANDARD NEW CABINETS

The most common dimensions for base cabinets are 36 inches high and 24 inches deep. Wall cabinets measure 12–30 inches high and 12 inches deep. Cabinet widths range from 9 to 48 inches.

speeds the production process. For the do-it-yourselfer, good results can be achieved using clear urethane. Urethane is tough and resistant to chemicals, and it can be applied easily with brushes.

REMOVING OLD CABINETS

Removing old cabinets, while not difficult, can be a messy and time-consuming job. Always take safety precautions with demolition work: Wear eye protection, leather gloves, and a hard hat.

Older modular cabinets that have been screwed together can be salvaged. Unscrew the cabinets and reuse them for basement or garage storage, or donate them to a charity. Save salvaged doors and drawers to dress up supplementary storage that you build yourself. If your old cabinets are built-in units or have been put together with nails and glue, the face frames probably will need to be cut into pieces for removal.

Metal cabinets usually attach to the wall with hangers. To remove the cabinets, loosen mounting screws from inside the cabinets, then lift the cabinets away from the wall. Then remove the hanger system.

Begin removal with either the upper or lower units. If you begin with the upper cabinets, you can use the lowers for support. If you start with the base units, you'll have more room to access the upper ones.

TOOLS

Flat pry bar, claw hammer, 4-inch putty knife, electric drill equipped with power screw tips, reciprocating saw or handsaw.

TOOL FACTS

A claw hammer has an appetite for demolition. The claw pulls nails and pries off trim. For prying tasks, look for a hammer with a straight or "ripping" claw and a steel or fiberglass handle. Wooden handles can break if they run into too much resistance.

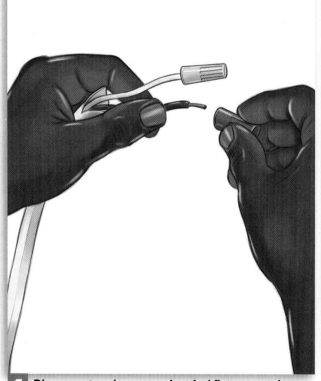

1 *Disconnect and remove electrical fixtures, such as undercabinet lighting or vent hoods. To do so, turn off the electrical power at the main service panel. Then disconnect wires and remove the fixtures. Cover loose wire ends with wire nuts before restoring power.*

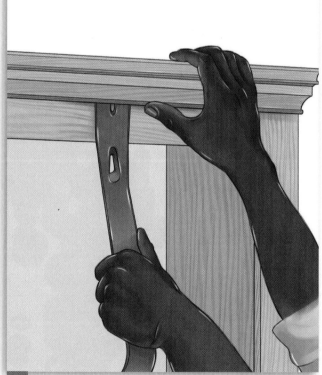

2 *Remove trim moldings at the tops of the upper cabinets using a flat pry bar and a claw hammer. Work carefully if you intend to salvage the moldings. Pry as closely as possible to nail locations to prevent breaking the molding.*

3 Remove valances—the decorative pieces that span between cabinets over windows. Some valances can be unscrewed from the inside edges of the face frames. If the valances have been nailed in place, you'll need to pry them loose or cut them apart for removal.

4 Remove vinyl base trim from cabinet toe kicks. Use a flat pry bar or putty knife to pry up a portion of the molding, then peel the remainder away from the cabinet. Remove any wooden base moldings with a flat pry bar.

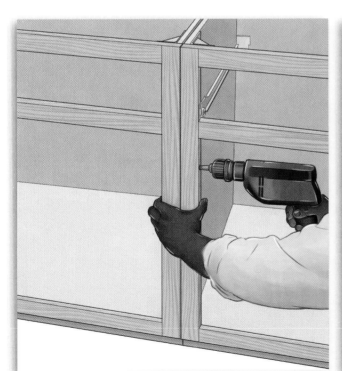

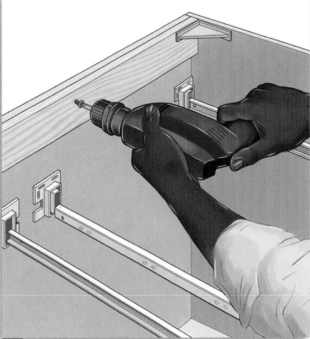

5 Remove all doors and drawers. Unscrew decorative sink front panels from inside sink cabinets. Remove any screws holding modular cabinet face frames together. These screws are located at the inside edges of the face frames. If the cabinets are fastened together with nails, cut the face frames apart with a handsaw or reciprocating saw.

6 At the back of the cabinets, remove any screws that fasten the units to the walls. If the cabinets are nailed to the walls, use a flat pry bar to pry the units away from the walls. Don't pry directly against wall surfaces. Instead, pry against a piece of scrap lumber inserted between the tool and the wall. Cut face frames apart with a handsaw or reciprocating saw.

PREPARING FOR NEW CABINETS

Installing cabinets is not a difficult task, but the job is easiest if old cabinets and appliances are stripped completely from the kitchen. (*To remove old cabinets, see pages 72–73.*) If you plan to change the electrical or plumbing systems, rough-in the new pipes, wires, outlets, and switches while the kitchen is empty, before the new cabinets go in.

In most cases, you'll want to install new flooring after the cabinets are in place. This sequence prevents accidental damage to the flooring surfaces. However, if your new flooring is thick, such as ceramic tile installed over a backer board underlayment, this sequence may cause problems. You might find that the new flooring is so thick that it prevents appliances, such as a refrigerator or dishwasher, from sliding into their positions. Before beginning cabinet installation, you'll need to determine if the thickness of new flooring is a potential problem. If so, you'll want to install base cabinets on shim material such as 1×3 boards laid flat. This will allow you to install flooring into the appliance locations and maintain proper clearances for the height of the appliances. Shim material must support the front, back, and sides of all base cabinets and should not extend beyond the edge of the toe kick.

The keys to a successful installation: Prepare the walls and floors, and create layout reference lines. Most rooms have slightly uneven surfaces—high spots in the floors or walls that aren't perfectly square. These imperfections won't be a problem if you identify their locations and take them into account during installation.

Reference lines ensure the cabinets are installed correctly so that doors and drawers operate smoothly and countertops are level.

TOOLS
Electronic stud finder, 4-foot level, electric drill equipped with power screw tips, tape measure.

TOOL FACTS
Electronic stud finders are handy and inexpensive battery-powered tools. You can find one at a home-improvement center for less than $15. A stud finder uses sound waves to pinpoint the location of dense material—wooden wall studs—beneath wallboard. This simple tool is highly accurate and easy to use.

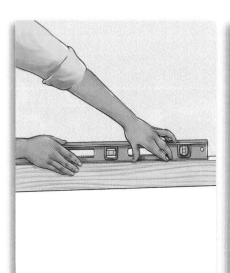

1 Use a long, straight 2×4 and a level to determine any high or low spots in the walls and floors where cabinets will run. Mark high spots for reference. Fill in any large depressions in walls with wallboard joint compound.

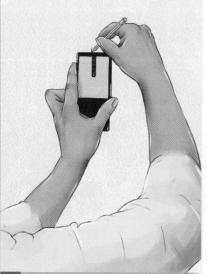

2 Use a stud finder to locate wall studs and mark their location for reference. The cabinets will be attached to wall studs with screws.

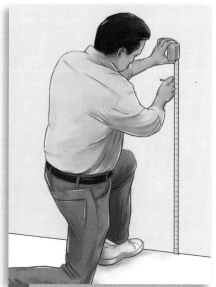

3 From the reference mark that indicates the high spot of your floors, measure up 34½ inches. When making this measurement, your tape measure should be held plumb. Mark the wall at this height.

4 *Use a 4-foot level to extend a horizontal base cabinet reference line completely around the room where the tops of the lower cabinets will be installed. If your runs are not continuous, you will have to repeat Step 3 for each run of cabinets. Frequently check the distance from the horizontal line to the floor. The distance must not be less than 34 ½ inches.*

5 *From the base cabinet reference line, measure up and mark at 19 ½ inches. This will be the bottom of the upper cabinets. Use a 4-foot level to extend a horizontal line completely around the room where upper cabinets will be installed. Check the distance between the two lines frequently to ensure it is 19 ½ inches.*

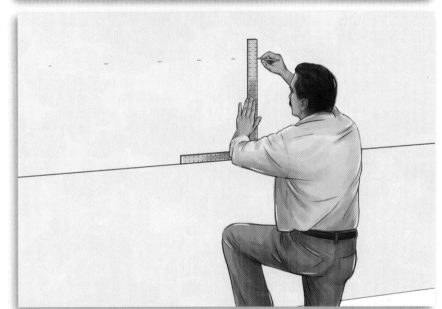

6 *Use 2 ½-inch drywall screws to install 1×3 ledgers with top edge flush to the line for the upper cabinets. This ledger will temporarily carry the weight of the upper cabinets during installation and will be removed after installation is complete. Transfer stud location marks to the ledger for reference.*

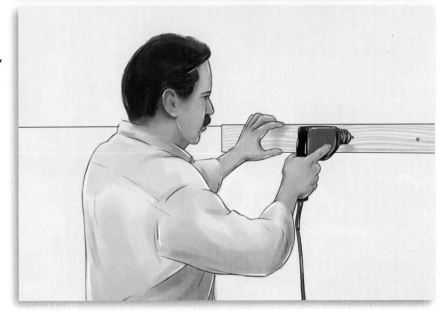

INSTALLING NEW CABINETS

Cabinet installation is basically a three-step process. First, the runs of cabinets are attached to the walls but not too tightly. Then, adjacent cabinets are fastened to each other. Finally, the runs are secured tightly to the walls.

Leaving the cabinets slightly loose from walls permits you to line up cabinet tops and face-frame surfaces. It also allows for any unevenness in walls and floors. For upper cabinets, a temporary 1×3 ledger helps support the weight of the cabinets until the entire run is hung on the walls. Once the cabinets are attached firmly to each other they can be secured tightly to the walls. Any unevenness in walls and floors is accounted for with shims placed behind the cabinets.

For installation, remove all cabinet doors and drawers. This makes the units lighter and prevents doors or drawers from opening and interfering with the process. Begin with the upper cabinet runs, and install corner units first. Lifting and positioning cabinets can be awkward. It's easier and safer if two people work together.

To fasten cabinets to each other, use No. 10 flathead wood screws that are long enough to reach through the edges of one face frame and penetrate at least ¾ inch into the adjacent face frame. Predrill holes for screws using a counterbore bit designed to provide a countersink hole for the heads of the screws. Clamp face frames together when drilling holes and driving screws to prevent the cabinets from shifting alignment.

For frameless cabinets (sometimes called European cabinets), join the units together with screws driven directly through the cabinet sides. Use 1¼-inch flathead wood screws and collar washers. Use at least four screws to secure adjacent cabinets.

Some manufacturers provide true corner cabinets. These units extend in two directions—when seen from above, the unit is V-shaped. These corner units are easy and straightforward to install. Most manufacturers, however, make blind corner cabinets. Blind units are actually two cabinets designed so that one butts into the other to form a right angle. The blind unit is installed first.

It's a good idea to test-fit blind units before installation to make sure doors and handles swing free and clear. You can test-fit the units on the ground, using a framing square to align

them. If necessary, install a filler strip between the cabinets to create the necessary clearance. Filler strips are usually 3–4 inches wide and are finished to match the cabinets. They are attached to the cabinet face frames with screws. Most manufacturers provide filler strips with your cabinet order. Make sure you have several on hand, and attach filler strips before beginning cabinet installation.

When you are satisfied with the alignment of your corner units, mark the location of the butted cabinet on the blind cabinet frame. That way, when you hoist the cabinets onto the ledger to begin installation, you can align them quickly and accurately.

Filler strips also are used when a run of cabinets butts directly into a wall. If the fit is not perfect, use a filler strip to make up the difference. Cover any gaps between the strip and the wall with molding.

TOOLS

Measuring tape, level, electric drill equipped with power screw tips, clamps, utility knife, counterbore bit.

INSTALLING UPPER CABINETS

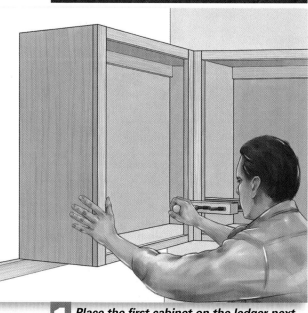

1 *Place the first cabinet on the ledger next to the wall. At corners, the first unit will be a blind cabinet. Butt the cabinet that begins the perpendicular run to the blind unit and clamp the two cabinets together.*

2 Drill pilot holes through the back of the cabinet into the studs. Use the stud markings on the ledger to drill holes accurately. Attach the cabinets to the walls using 2½-inch panhead screws and collar washers, but do not tighten the screws completely. Leave about ¼ inch of play at the back of the cabinets until all the units are installed.

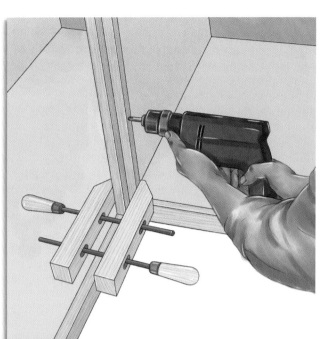

3 Fasten face frames together by drilling pilot holes with a counterbore bit through the edges of the face frames. Use No. 10 flathead wood screws that are long enough to reach through the edges of face frames and penetrate at least ¾ inch into the adjacent face frame.

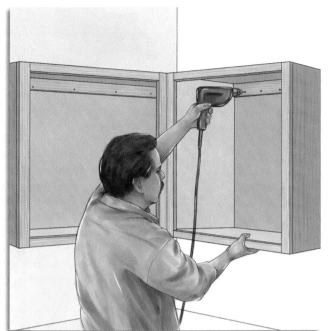

4 Position and clamp the next cabinet in the run. Secure it loosely to walls studs using 2½-inch panhead wood screws and collar washers. Fasten face frames together as described in Step 3. When the entire run is secured to the wall, remove the temporary ledger. Use a level to check the face frames for plumb. If necessary, install wooden shims at the backs of the cabinets. Tighten screws completely.

5 Use a utility knife to cut off exposed shims. Cover any gaps between the cabinets and the wall with trim. Where decorative valances are installed over sinks, measure the distance between the cabinets. Cut valance to length. Clamp valance in place and attach with screws from inside edges of cabinet face frames. Complete the upper cabinets by installing all doors.

INSTALLING NEW CABINETS
continued

INSTALLING LOWER CABINETS

Install lower cabinets using many of the same procedures you followed to install your upper cabinets. Begin with runs that include corner or blind units and install the blind units first. Careful installation at the corners ensures the remainder of the run is level and plumb.

If your layout includes appliances, such as a dishwasher or refrigerator, measure carefully to allow the proper spacing between cabinets. Use the manufacturer's guidelines for clearance at each side of the appliance. If clearance may be a problem, you can shim up lower cabinets before installing flooring (*see* "Preparing for New Cabinets," page 74).

TOOLS

Measuring tape, level, electric drill equipped with power screw tips, clamps, utility knife, jigsaw, counterbore bit.

1 *Install blind unit and make sure it is even with horizontal reference line on the wall. Check the front of the cabinet for plumb. Shim if necessary. Drill pilot holes through the back of the cabinet into the studs. Use the stud markings on the wall to drill holes accurately. Attach the cabinets to the walls, using 2½-inch panhead screws and collar washers. Leave about ¼ inch of play at the back of the cabinets until all the units are installed.*

2 *If necessary, install filler strips at corners. Butt adjacent corner cabinet to the blind unit. Make sure it is plumb and flush with the horizontal reference line on the wall. Shim if necessary. Clamp face frames together.*

3 *Fasten face frames together by drilling pilot holes with a counterbore bit through the edges of the face frames. Use No. 10 flathead wood screws that are long enough to reach through the edges of face frames and penetrate at least ¾ inch into the adjacent face frame.*

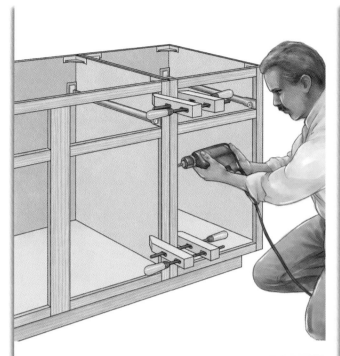

4 Position and clamp the next cabinet in the run. Secure it loosely to walls studs using 2½-inch panhead wood screws and collar washers. Fasten face frames together as described in Step 3.

5 Measure and mark the backs of cabinets for any plumbing pipes, heating vents, or access to electrical outlets. Cut openings with a jigsaw.

6 Position and clamp the next cabinet in the run. Secure it loosely to wall studs using 2½-inch panhead wood screws and collar washers. Fasten face frames together as described in Step 3. Check for level and plumb, shimming if necessary. When the entire run has been installed, tighten all screws. Cut off any exposed shims with a utility knife. Cover gaps between cabinets and flooring with trim.

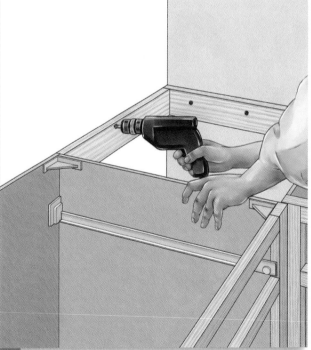

7 Some corner units do not extend all the way to the wall. If so, you'll need to install a permanent ledger to support the countertop. Cut 1×3 or other suitable material to length. Use 2½-inch wood screws or wallboard screws to fasten the ledger with its top edge flush with the horizontal reference line.

COUNTERTOPS

A new countertop can boost the appearance and function of your kitchen. And if you have a limited budget, this one change offers a dramatic facelift for the entire room. You'll find many kinds of countertop surfaces, each with its unique properties and price. Several of them are well-suited to do-it-yourself projects.

Good planning is key to successful installations. Some materials, such as granite, marble, and manufactured solid surfaces, may have to be ordered weeks in advance and require professional fabrication and installation. For these materials, you must know the sizes and rough-in dimensions for sinks and cooktops so they can be provided to the countertop fabricator prior to installation. To keep your project running smoothly, make as many decisions as possible in advance of installation. In addition to the type and color of the countertop material, you'll need to decide on the finish, edge treatment, corner style, and the type and height of the backsplash.

A MEASURE OF QUALITY

When working with professional fabricators and countertop installers, insist that they make the field measurements. If you take your own measurements for a do-it-yourself installation, follow these guidelines:
■ Measure only after all cabinets are installed.
■ Figure a 1-inch overhang in front of the cabinets and at open ends.
■ Figure a ⅛-inch overhang where the cabinets meet appliances.
■ Remember that walls often are not perfectly square to each other. When butting a countertop to an uneven or un-square wall, measure to the longest point. You can then carefully shape the countertop with a sander or hand plane to fit the wall surface.
■ Make all measurements twice.

Warm and versatile, wood makes a fine countertop surface in this sunny kitchen. These maple butcher-block countertops were sealed with polyurethane to protect against moisture and food stains.

CHOOSING MATERIALS

Durable laminates are available in hundreds of colors and textures to complement any design.

DECORATIVE LAMINATES

The most popular type of countertops, decorative laminates, are made of plastic resins pressed into sheets about ¹⁄₁₆ inch thick. The laminate is glued to a supporting substrate of plywood or particleboard.

Their popularity is easy to understand: Decorative laminates are durable, come in a wide range of colors and textures, and cost less than many alternatives. And installation makes a good do-it-yourself project. Purchase laminates with a matte finish. Gloss finishes look good but scratch easily, especially with everyday use. You have three options:

■ Buy sections of premade countertop and cut them to size.
■ Order a custom countertop, with or without installation.
■ Purchase the laminate separately and make your own top.

Premade laminate countertops, also called postformed countertops, are stocked in most home-improvement centers. The color selection is usually limited; backsplashes and edge treatments are fixed and cannot be customized; and the sections come in many lengths but only one width. If you order a custom top from a local fabricator, you can specify virtually any shape and color.

To save money, you can install a custom top yourself, but you'll have to arrange for delivery.

You'll save even more money if you decide to make the countertop yourself. This is not a difficult project, but it requires plenty of time and patience. Don't plan any mitered joints. Making a clean mitered joint is very difficult if you don't have the right equipment.

CERAMIC TILE

Tile makes a good do-it-yourself material for countertops and backsplashes, although getting professional results is a challenge for the first-time tile setter. Tile is durable and comes in many colors, sizes, and styles. It can be installed directly over an old laminated countertop as long as the laminate is undamaged and firmly attached to its substrate. Always use glazed ceramic tiles for countertops. Unglazed tiles can stain, especially around sinks or food preparation areas. Purchase tiles that are rated for horizontal surfaces. They're usually thicker and more durable than tiles made for walls.

Ceramic tile invites you to be creative. You can mix colors and textures or install decorative borders as part of the backsplash. A few expensive tiles, such as embossed or hand-painted tiles, can give a look of elegance at a relatively low overall cost.

GRANITE AND MARBLE

These expensive materials make exceptionally beautiful and durable countertops, but they warrant careful consideration. Marble will stain if not properly sealed. And natural stone is heavy and difficult to cut and shape, so it isn't recommended for do-it-yourselfers. Trust only experienced professionals.

Even if solid granite or marble countertops are beyond your budget, you may want to install a section of natural stone for a specialty food preparation area. Stone is favored by bakers who require a cool, non-porous surface for preparing dough. When installing a section of stone that will be butted to adjacent surfaces, such as a laminate countertop, take into consideration any difference in thicknesses of the two materials. You may have to shim the thinner material to maintain a level surface.

If you are planning to include a natural stone countertop in your kitchen, visit a stone dealer early in the process so you can determine prices, availability, and when to schedule installation. Make sure the dealer

PRICE COMPARISON

Material	Price per foot, installed
Decorative laminate	$ 25–50
Ceramic tile	$ 10–50
Granite and marble	$125–250
Solid-surface material	$100–250
Wood	$ 2–50

takes measurements, and be sure to provide dimensions and exact locations of sinks and appliances so that the dealer can make the proper cutouts. Square stone edges can be sharp, so specify softened edges and rounded corners.

SOLID-SURFACE COUNTERTOPS

You can get many advantages of stone with few of the drawbacks in countertops cast from acrylic resins. This solid-surface material requires little maintenance, is very durable, and comes in a variety of colors. Minor scorch marks, scratches, and abrasions can be removed with fine-grade sandpaper. The methods and tools used for working with solid-surface materials are similar to those used for wood. However, most manufacturers will guarantee the material only if it is installed professionally.

WOOD COUNTERTOPS

Attractive wood surfaces make great food preparation surfaces and are relatively easy to install. They usually are made of hardwood strips laminated to form a "butcher's block" that is 1–1½ inches thick. Wood is a porous material, however, and prone to water damage and staining, so it is a poor choice for areas near sinks. Butcher-block tops are ideal for island counters.

ABOVE: *Tile has been used in homes for centuries. In the kitchen, tile is unsurpassed for its beauty and durability.*

LEFT: *Solid surface materials are easy-to-clean and impervious to stains.*

FAR LEFT: *Marble or granite countertops offer rare beauty; they are also expensive.*

LEFT: *Wood countertops provide food preparation surfaces throughout the kitchen.*

OUT WITH THE OLD

To remove old countertops, you'll first need to turn off the water supply to any fixtures and then disconnect plumbing lines. If your plumbing lines are equipped with shutoff valves, turn off the water at the valves. If not, you'll have to shut off the main water supply. After you do so, you may want to install shutoff valves so that you can restore water to the rest of your house while you replace your countertops and fixtures.

Before you begin, you must disconnect any electrical connections for built-in cooktops or downdraft ventilation systems. Always shut off power at the service panel and test connections for current with a voltage tester before proceeding.

TOOLS

For all tasks: Adjustable wrench, flat pry bar, screwdriver, reciprocating saw, utility knife.
For ceramic tile countertop removal: Cold chisel, hammer, circular saw with a masonry-cutting blade.

TOOL FACTS

A cold chisel, sometimes called a masonry chisel, is made especially for breaking apart hard objects, such as stone, brick, and tile. It is made of a single piece of forged steel and has a cutting end that is beveled but not sharpened. The other end is made to be hit with a hammer. The cold chisel is a tough tool but shouldn't be used for lifting or prying. Always wear eye protection when using a cold chisel for breaking apart materials.

A masonry-cutting blade is an abrasive disk that fits on a circular saw. It is made especially to cut hard materials, such as stone, brick, and tile. For safety, it is usually best to make several shallow cuts rather than one deep cut. That way, there is less resistance at the cutting edge of the blade and the saw is easier to control. Try a blade depth of about ¼ inch. Always wear eye protection when using a masonry blade to cut materials apart.

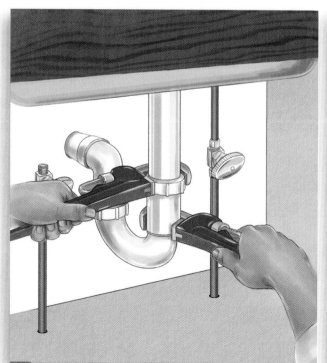

1 *Disconnect and remove plumbing fixtures and appliances. Shut off power before disconnecting and removing electrical appliances.*

2 *Locate and remove any brackets or screws holding the countertop to the cabinets. These fasteners will be accessible from underneath the countertop. Leave corner blocks or braces in place.*

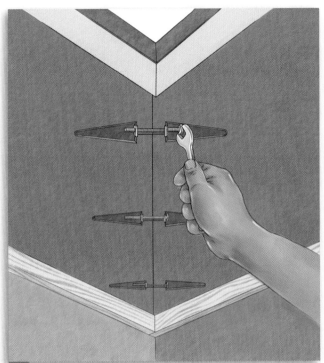

3 *From underneath the countertops, unscrew take-up bolts that join mitered corners together.*

4 *Use a utility knife to cut caulk at the backsplash and edges of the countertops. Pry off trim. Use a pry bar to lift the countertop away from the cabinets.*

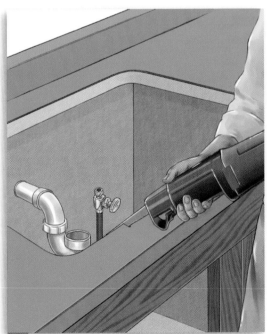

5 *If the countertop is too heavy to lift or if it is nailed in place, you may have to cut it apart to make removal easier. Use a reciprocating saw equipped with a metal-cutting blade to cut the countertop into pieces, and make the cuts at the sink cutout location. Protect the cabinet as you cut the countertop.*

REMOVE TILE

To remove old ceramic tile countertops, you'll first need to remove the tile. Wear protective glasses or safety goggles. Use a cold chisel, sometimes called a masonry chisel, to break up the tile. If your tile counter has a masonry bed, you'll need to cut apart the bed with a circular saw equipped with a masonry-cutting blade. Take care not to damage the base cabinets.

INSTALLING A LAMINATE COUNTERTOP

Postformed laminate countertops are available readily at home-improvement centers. They come in stock lengths that are cut to fit your cabinets, and they can be purchased with mitered corners. They include a rolled front edge and a seamless backsplash. At the top of the backsplash, there is a small overhang called a scribing strip. Adjusting the scribing strip will create a tight fit against uneven walls. You'll need an endcap kit to cover unfinished countertop ends with laminate.

When cutting a postformed countertop to length, you'll need space to work. Setting up a couple of sawhorses in a garage is a good idea. Since you'll be turning the countertop upside down to cut it, remember to protect the laminate from scratches by placing a dropcloth or pieces of cardboard between the countertop and the sawhorses.

To help prevent chipping the laminate, the method described here calls for cutting out holes for sinks and appliances prior to positioning the countertop on the base cabinets. Because this method weakens the countertop, carefully handle the sections. Sections of countertop are awkward to handle anyway, so it's wise to recruit a friend to help lift and carry.

TOOLS

Measuring tape, adjustable wrench, framing square, straightedge guide (a straight piece of 1×4 wood will do), clamps, jigsaw, electric drill with power screw tips, belt sander, file, household iron, compass, caulk gun, level.

TOOL FACTS

Many jigsaws are equipped with adjustment switches that change the blade action from vigorous, coarse strokes to fine, delicate strokes. For cutting laminate, choose a finer stroke to prevent chipping. Be sure to use a fine-toothed wood-cutting or metal-cutting blade. Metal-cutting blades will work on wood, but they cut at a slower rate than wood-cutting blades. Turn the workpiece so that the laminate surface is on the bottom as you cut.

The compass you select can be of the simple variety often used by grade school children. Be sure the pencil is sharp and the action of the compass is stiff—the metal arc should fit tightly to the pencil holder. That way, the setting will not change as you use the tool.

1 *Measure the length of your base cabinets. Add 1 inch for all exposed cabinet ends. If the countertop will butt against an appliance, add only ⅛ inch.*

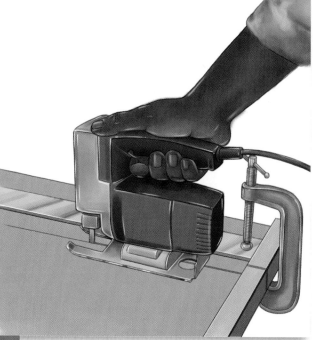

2 *Use a framing square to mark cutting lines on the bottom of the countertop. Clamp a straightedge to the countertop to use as a guide, then cut off the excess with a jigsaw equipped with a fine-toothed wood-cutting blade. Cutting from the bottom will prevent the teeth of the saw blade from chipping the laminate.*

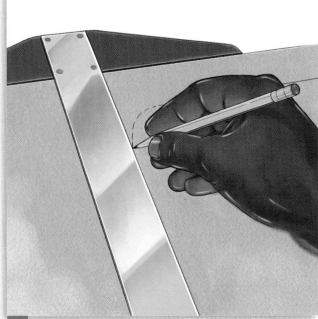

3 Mark locations for any sinks or appliances. Most sinks and appliances come with rough-in dimensions for the hole sizes they require. Carefully draw these dimensions on the bottom of the countertop. As with any measurement, always check your work.

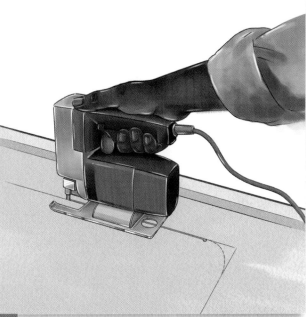

4 Just inside the cutout lines, drill a pilot hole that is big enough to accommodate the jigsaw blade. Cut along the lines with a jigsaw. Make sure that waste material is supported from below so that it doesn't sag or fall before the cutting is complete. If it does, it is likely to break or tear the laminate surface.

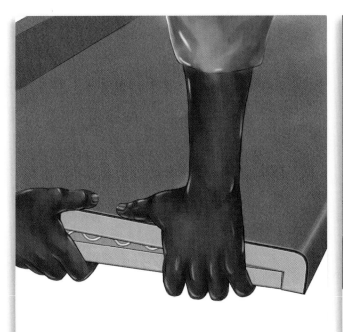

5 Exposed ends of the countertop should be covered with laminate from the endcap kit. First, build up the thickness of the unfinished end by fastening a ¾-inch by ¾-inch batten to the underside of the countertop, using carpenter's glue. When the glue is dry, sand off any unevenness with a belt sander.

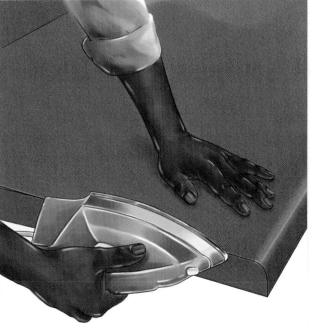

6 The endcap should be slightly larger than the end. Position it so the amount of excess is equal in all directions. Activate the adhesive with a household iron set at medium heat. Remove excess laminate by filing the endcap flush to the countertop. To avoid chipping, file in only one direction—toward the countertop.

INSTALLING A LAMINATE COUNTERTOP
continued

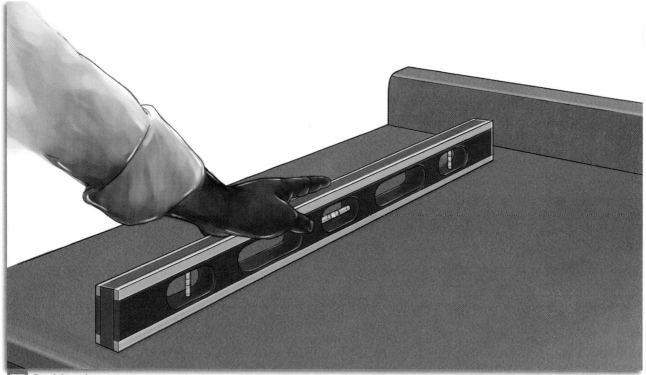

7 Position the countertop on the base cabinets. Check the countertop to make sure it is level. Make sure all doors and drawers open freely. If necessary, adjust the countertop height with wood shims.

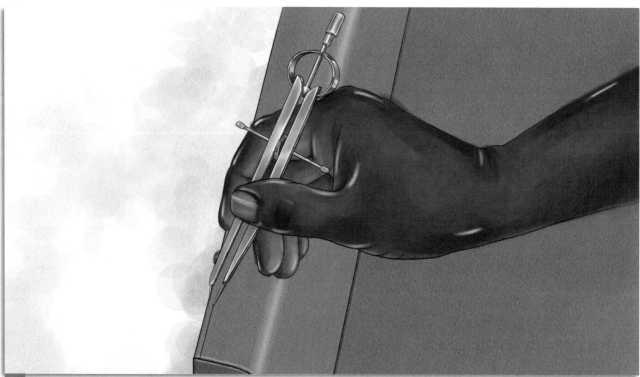

8 Use a compass to transfer any unevenness in the walls to the scribing strip—the top edge of the backsplash that faces the wall. Set the compass so that the distance between the metal point and the point of the pencil is equal to the distance of the largest gap you see between the scribing strip and the wall. With the metal tip against the wall, draw the compass along the length of the backsplash, letting the pencil tip draw a line on the scribing strip.

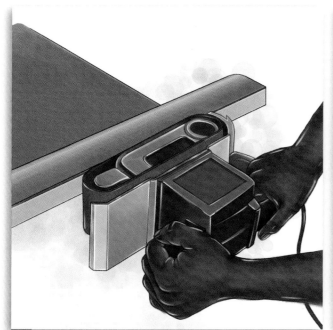

9 Position the countertop on a pair of sawhorses and use a belt sander to remove the excess from the scribing strip. Set the countertop back in place. Any minor gaps that still exist will be covered by silicone caulk (step 12).

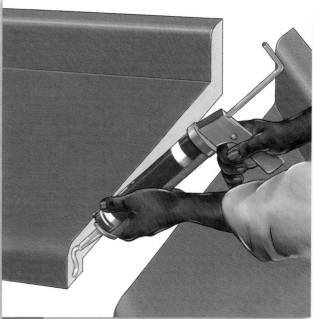

10 At mitered corners, first "dry fit" the pieces and make all necessary adjustments. Then apply a bead of silicone caulk along the inside of the mitered edges. Bring the mitered pieces together, then tighten them from underneath, using miter take-up bolts. As you tighten the bolts, make sure the top surfaces are flush.

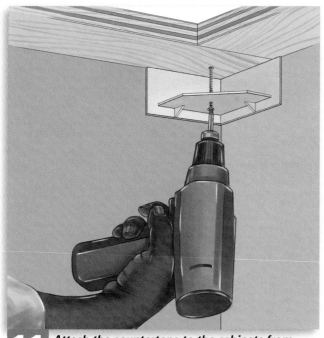

11 Attach the countertops to the cabinets from underneath by driving wallboard screws up through corner brackets. Use screws long enough to penetrate at least ½ inch into the countertop substrate but not long enough to pierce the top of the laminate.

12 Use silicone caulk to seal the seam between the backsplash and the wall. Smooth the silicone bead with a wet fingertip and wipe away excess caulk.

INSTALLING A CERAMIC TILE COUNTERTOP

Installing a ceramic tile countertop can be a fun do-it-yourself project that rewards careful planning. Because the size of the tiles, together with the width of the grout lines, rarely works out to be an exact match for the size of the countertop, you will probably have to cut and install partial tiles. Deciding exactly where to place the full and the partial tiles will ensure that the finished layout looks good.

Ceramic tile can be installed over old laminate surfaces if the laminates are in good condition and firmly bonded to their substrate. Remember that adding tile slightly raises the sinks and fixtures, so you'll need to adjust the plumbing.

For new countertops, ceramic tile can be installed directly on a ¾-inch plywood core. For protection against moisture, buy exterior-grade plywood that is free of holes or voids.

Another installation method uses a ½-inch-thick cement backer board placed over a ¾-inch plywood core. Backer board, also called a glass mesh mortar unit (GMMU), is made specifically for use under ceramic tile. It can be cut to size by scoring it with a utility knife and snapping the piece along the scored line, or by using a circular saw equipped with a carbide-tipped blade. Installing backer board over plywood makes a stable and waterproof foundation for ceramic

tile. It's well worth the extra time and expense, so that's the method described on these pages.

You'll need to consider the size and shape of the edge tiles when creating your layout. Edge tiles come in a variety of shapes. Some are flat with rounded edges, called bullnose tiles. Others, called V-cap tiles, are formed in right angles to completely cover edges.

You'll need to know the vertical measurement of the finished edge, taking into account the edge tile and the thickness of the core materials. Then, measure to make sure the edge tiles won't interfere with drawers or cabinet doors. If so, you'll need to shim up the countertop by nailing pieces of plywood along the rim of the base cabinets.

TOOLS

- Measuring tape
- Putty knife
- Electric drill (with screw tips)
- Screwdriver
- Framing square
- Tile cutter
- Tile nippers
- Notched trowel
- Caulk gun
- Hammer
- Grout float
- Grout sponge

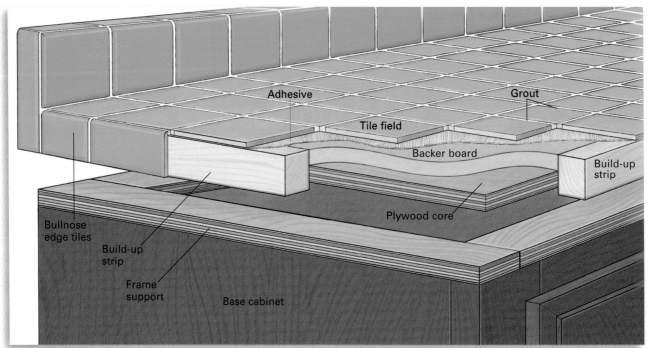

Properly supported ceramic tile offers a countertop surface that is durable, beautiful, and easy to clean. Take time to arrange tiles for a balanced appearance.

Equal rows of large partial tiles on both sides will look better than a full row on one side and a narrow sliver on the other.

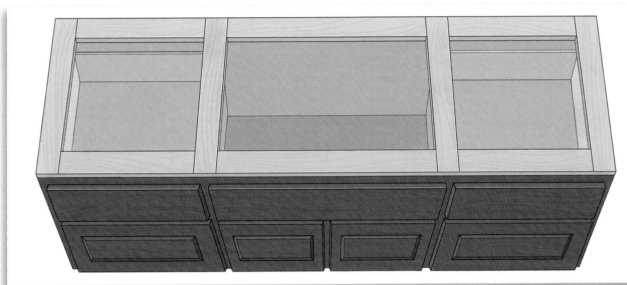

1 Cut 3-inch wide frame supports from ¾-inch exterior grade plywood. Fasten the supports around the top perimeter of the base cabinet and every 24 inches across the cabinet, using galvanized 4d common nails. Install frame supports across cabinets about 3 inches from the sides of sink and cooktop locations.

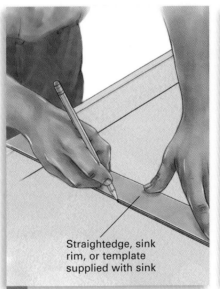

Straightedge, sink rim, or template supplied with sink

2 Cut core materials to the same size as the base cabinet unit. Use ¾-inch exterior grade plywood topped with ½-inch cement backer board. Position the core materials flush to all edges and fasten them to the frame supports with galvanized 2-inch wallboard screws. Fill cracks and screw holes in the backer board with latex underlayment. When the underlayment is dry, sand it flush with the surrounding surfaces.

3 Mark the location of sinks and cooktops. Cut out holes according to the rough-in dimensions provided by the manufacturer. To cut backer board, wear eye protection and use a circular saw equipped with a carbide-tipped blade. For safety, make several passes, setting the blade deeper with each pass. Support waste material from underneath to prevent tear-out. If you are installing a recessed sink, set it in place now. Surface-mounted sinks are installed after all tiling.

4 To make a base for edge tiles and an overhang, install 1×2 build-up strips of pine or exterior grade plywood along the exposed edges of the countertop core. Attach the strips, using carpenter's glue and galvanized 6d finish nails. The build-up strips should be flush with the top of the core.

INSTALLING A CERAMIC TILE COUNTERTOP
continued

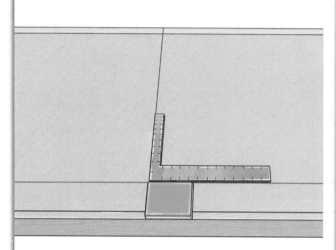

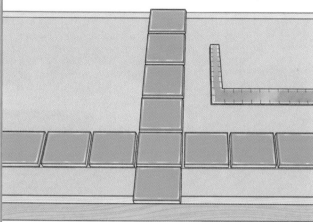

5 *Measure and mark the middle of the countertop core. Place a full tile along this center line and flush to the edge of the build-up strip. Use a framing square to establish perpendicular lines that extend to all edges of the core. If you are using V-cap edge tiles, you'll need to begin with an edge tile, leave grout spacing, then place a full tile against the layout lines.*

6 *Dry fit a row of tiles along the perpendicular lines, using plastic grout spacers between the tiles. If necessary, adjust the layout lines or the grout spaces. Pre-cut any partial tiles to make installation easier. When measuring for partial tiles, be sure to account for grout lines. Where tiles butt against wall surface, allow ⅛ inch of space or the thickness of one tile.*

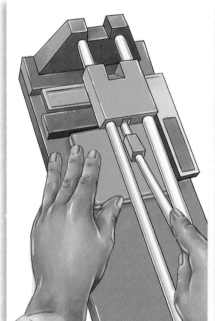

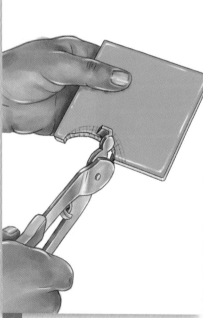

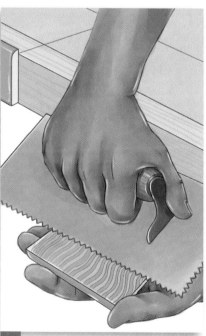

7 *For straight cuts, place the tile face-up in a tile cutter. Adjust the tool to the correct width, then score the tile by pulling the cutter wheel across the tile. Snap the tile by applying pressure according to directions supplied with the cutter.*

8 *For curved cuts, score an outline of the curve with a tile scoring tool. Use the scoring tool to cover the waste portion with crisscrossed lines. Use tile nippers to break off small pieces of the waste material until the cutout is complete.*

9 *Begin setting tiles at the edge: The rounded top of bullnose tiles should be set flush to the surface of the field tiles, so place a loose tile along the build-up strips for reference. Apply a thin layer of tile adhesive to the edge of the countertop and build-up strip using a notched trowel. Press the tiles into place with a slight twist.*

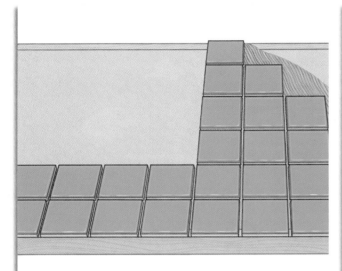

10 Spread adhesive along the front of the countertop core and install a row of full tiles. Then install a perpendicular row of tiles along the layout lines. Work small areas at a time, alternating perpendicular rows. Use denatured alcohol to remove adhesive from the face of tiles before the adhesive dries.

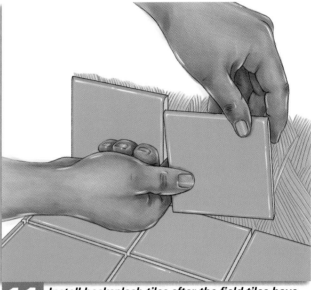

11 Install backsplash tiles after the field tiles have been completely installed. Leave ¹⁄₁₆ to ⅛ inch of space between the bottom of the backsplash tiles and the field tiles. This joint should not be grouted. Instead, seal it with silicone caulk after the tile installation is complete (see step 14).

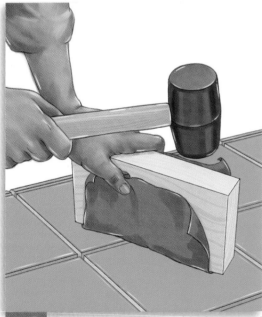

12 Set the tiles with a 2×4 block wrapped in carpet or a towel. Place the block on the tiles and gently tap the block with a hammer or mallet. Use a toothpick to remove the plastic grout spacers.

13 Mix grout and apply with a rubber grout float. Use a sweeping motion to force the grout into the spaces between the tiles. Wipe away excess grout with a damp sponge. Grout sponges have rounded edges that prevent the sponge from lifting the grout out of the joints. After the grout has dried completely according to the manufacturer's instructions, seal the grout with two coats of a penetrating liquid silicone sealer. Let dry, then buff the tiles with a soft cloth.

14 Seal joints around the backsplash with silicone caulk. Smooth the bead with a wet fingertip and wipe away the excess.

INSTALLING PLUMBING FIXTURES AND APPLIANCES

Homeowners took advantage of this small kitchen alcove by installing a new stove, vent hood, and tile surround. It's a true kitchen remodeling in a very small space.

Installing new appliances and fixtures is relatively simple, especially if you are removing older appliances and replacing them with new ones of similar shapes and sizes. Measure appliances carefully to determine if they will fit in the available spaces. If you are moving appliances to different locations, installing additional appliances, or switching between electricity and gas, you'll need to rough-in any plumbing, gas lines, or new electrical outlets and circuits (see "Roughing-in," pages 28–31). Licensed electricians and plumbers will ensure the new work gets done properly and conforms to local building codes.

Installing some appliances and fixtures, such as sinks, faucets, and food disposers, makes good do-it-yourself projects. It's important to study the diagrams and directions on these pages to gain a thorough knowledge of the process before you begin. That way, you can have all the parts and tools on hand and won't have to shut off your electricity or water supply for longer than necessary.

Take a lesson in plumbing from the kitchen sink. Most base cabinets allow reasonable access to the sink's plumbing. And the sink is like a training lab for other plumbing work. Most of the essential elements are there: pipes and fittings, traps and drains, hot and cold water lines, faucets and valves.... For a do-it-yourselfer, a sink installation offers a real opportunity to get your feet wet.

Replacing the countertop, adding a rimmed stainless steel sink, and painting the old cabinets create a new look for this kitchen.

Some plumbing projects have nothing to do with remodeling. This kitchen needed a water line to serve a new refrigerator's ice-maker.

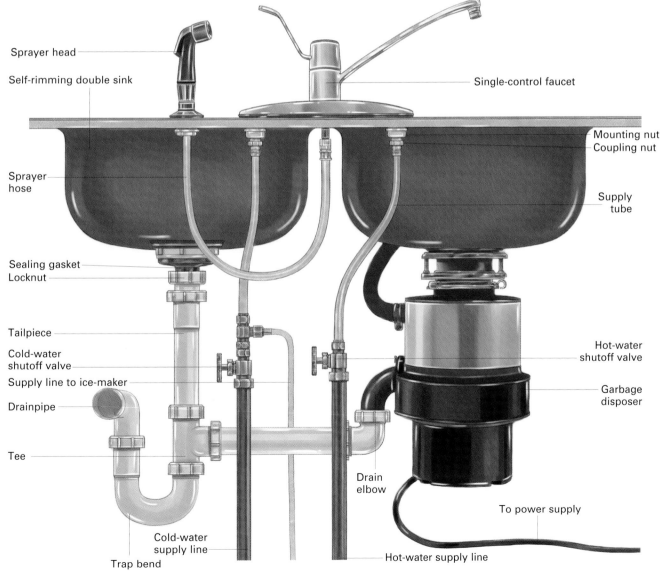

Sprayer head

Self-rimming double sink

Single-control faucet

Mounting nut
Coupling nut

Sprayer hose

Supply tube

Sealing gasket
Locknut

Tailpiece

Hot-water shutoff valve

Cold-water shutoff valve

Supply line to ice-maker

Garbage disposer

Drainpipe

Tee

Drain elbow

To power supply

Cold-water supply line

Trap bend

Hot-water supply line

INSTALLING A SINK

The owners of this kitchen employed cost-saving ideas by installing a new faucet to dress up an older rimmed, stainless steel sink.

In the hardworking world of kitchens, sinks make a real splash. They're available in any shape, color, and configuration you can imagine. Home-improvement centers usually have a good selection on hand or have catalogs to help you select a custom look. For even more choices, visit a kitchen specialty store or kitchen design center. Special orders—unusual shapes or custom colors—may require up to six weeks for delivery, so allow time in your remodeling plans.

When shopping, consider how many holes your faucets require. Most kitchen faucet sets call for three holes, but you may need another hole for a sprayer (*see page 86–87*) or an air gap for a dishwasher (*see pages 90-91*).

Sinks most often are made from stainless steel, cast-iron, or synthetic materials. Each differs in attributes and appearance, and each will vary in quality and price. When comparison

shopping, be sure to check specifications and the manufacturer's warranty.

■ **STAINLESS STEEL** is light, durable, and relatively inexpensive. The look is popular with homeowners who may have other stainless steel appliances. A high nickel content in the steel helps prevent corrosion, and a high chrome content provides a durable, easy-to-clean finish. Brushed chrome finishes hide scratches and other small imperfections much better than polished, mirrorlike finishes. The thickness of the steel is rated by number; the lower the number, the thicker the material. Steel rated 20-gauge is inexpensive, but the thin steel can sound tinny when items are moved inside the sink. Steel rated 18-gauge is stronger and quieter. Some stainless steel sinks also come with an undercoating that helps muffle sound.

■ **ENAMELED CAST IRON** is the most popular type of sink, although good quality tends to be expensive. It is heavy, durable, and extremely resistant to stains and scratches. One of the most attractive features is the variety of colors available. A custom-color enameled sink can be the focal point of any kitchen. Large enameled cast-iron sinks are very heavy and should be installed carefully.

■ **COMPOSITE AND SYNTHETIC** sinks are made of various materials, such as resins, ground quartz, polyester, acrylic, and silica. Usually, the greater the percentage of quartz in the formula, the harder the sink will be.

Solid surface countertops can be integrated with sinks of the same material. The result, a seamless work center, makes cleanup a snap.

These sinks are tough, durable, relatively lightweight, and quiet. They also are expensive and do not come in a wide variety of colors. Much of their appeal comes from the fact that they have a nontraditional look. Some are made from the same synthetic materials as solid-surface countertops. These sinks often are blended seamlessly into the countertop to make cleanup extremely easy.

TOOLS

Utility knife, screwdriver, basin wrench, plumber's wrench.

TOOL FACTS

A basin wrench has a long, slim handle and is made specifically to reach into hard-to-reach places and loosen or tighten nuts of various sizes. It is an especially helpful tool for unscrewing stubborn nuts, such as coupling nuts from underneath sinks. Although a specialty tool, it is not expensive and makes a good addition to a homeowner's tool kit.

A cast-iron undermount sink works well with tile countertops. It's easy to sweep debris directly into the sink's double bowls.

MOUNTING METHODS

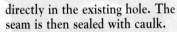

Three types of sinks have distinct mounting methods, each easily undertaken by the do-it-yourselfer.
■ **SELF-RIMMING SINKS** have thick, rolled edges designed to sit on the counter. This popular style is especially good for simple retrofitting projects—after removing an old sink you can set a new self-rimming sink

directly in the existing hole. The seam is then sealed with caulk.
■ **RIMMED SINKS** attach with a metal band that covers the perimeter of the sink cutout. This mounting method allows the sink to be installed almost flush with the countertop and allows spills to be swept into the sink for easy cleanup.

■ **UNDERMOUNT SINKS** are attached beneath the countertop using clips. Because the edge of the countertop is exposed, this method works especially well with tiled countertops, where the edge can be covered by edge tiles, or with solid-surface countertops, where the color and pattern of the material extend throughout its thickness.

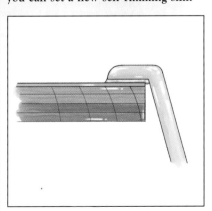

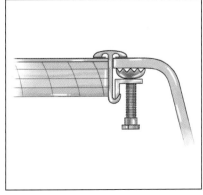

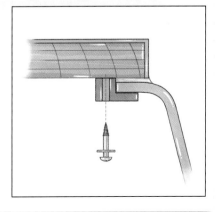

INSTALLING A SINK
continued

REMOVING OLD SINKS

SELF-RIMMING SINKS:
Use a utility knife to cut the caulk between the sink and countertop. Remove the strainers from the sink by unscrewing the locknut from underneath. With the strainers removed, grasp the sink through the drain holes and lift it out. Avoid prying the sink out, as the force may damage the countertop surface. If the sink is cast iron, two people may be needed to remove it.

RIMMED OR UNDERMOUNT SINKS: Inspect the sink from underneath to determine the types of fasteners used. Then remove all fasteners and clips with a screwdriver. Remove the strainers from the sink by unscrewing the locknut from underneath. With the strainers removed, grasp the sink through the drain holes and lift it out. Avoid prying out the sink as the force required may damage the countertop surface permanently.

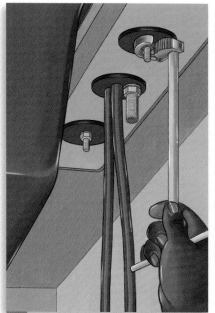

1 *Turn off the water supply by closing the shutoff valves under the sink. If your supply tubes are not equipped with shutoff valves, shut off the water at the main valve located near your water meter. Remove the supply tubes from the faucet tailpieces by unscrewing the coupling nuts. If necessary, use a basin wrench. If the supply tubes are soldered to the tailpieces, you will have to cut them.*

2 *Place a bucket underneath the waste trap to catch excess water. Remove the trap and drain tailpiece by unscrewing the slip nuts.*

INSTALLING A SELF-RIMMING SINK

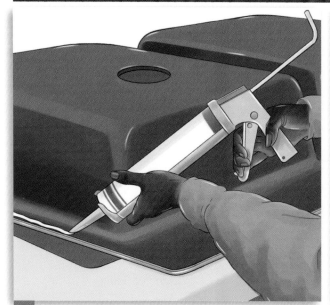

1 *Turn the new sink upside down. Apply a bead of silicone caulk completely around the rim of the sink.*

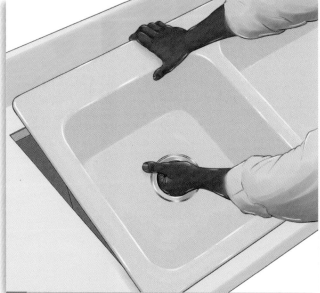

2 *Turn the sink over, taking care not to smear the caulk. Grasp the sink through the drain holes and lower it into position. Wipe away excess caulk with a damp rag.*

INSTALLING A RIMMED SINK

1 *Place the metal sink rim upside down on a flat surface. Apply a bead of silicone caulk on the inside of the rim.*

2 *Set the sink upside down into the frame. Use a flat-blade screwdriver to bend the tabs that fasten the rim to the sink. Set the sink and rim into the cutout hole in the countertop.*

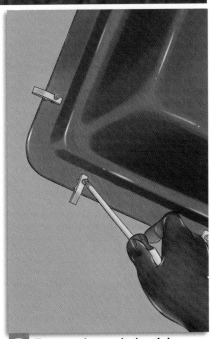

3 *From underneath the sink, install mounting clips every 8 inches around the rim. Tighten the mounting clips to secure the sink in the cutout hole.*

INSTALLING AN UNDERMOUNT SINK

HELPFUL TIPS

The key to success with an undermount sink is to hold it in place while securing it from underneath using the mounting clips provided by the sink manufacturer. This is a difficult task for one person; two are recommended. To make the job easier, support the sink from underneath while you work. A helpful tool is a scissors-type car jack. Place a piece of scrap wood between the sink bottom and the jack to prevent damage to the sink, then raise the sink into position. If the jack is not tall enough when extended, stack lumber under the jack stand. Raise the sink just until it's snug to the underside of the counter.

1 *Set the sink right-side up on a level surface. Apply a bead of silicone caulk to the sink's top edge.*

2 *Position the sink under the countertop and press into place. From underneath, screw the mounting clips every 8 inches around the sink's edge.*

INSTALLING A FAUCET AND SPRAYER

Kitchen faucets come in two forms. Those without supply tubes have three tailpieces—one for hot water hookup, one for cold, and a central tailpiece for a sprayer. Mounting nuts that screw onto the hot and cold tailpieces secure the faucet to the sink. The tailpieces are attached to the plumbing supply shutoff valves under the sink via flexible supply tubes. Another type of faucet has copper supply tubes attached to the faucet body and a threaded tailpiece at the center of the base for attaching a sprayer. The copper tubes and center tailpiece must be inserted through the center mounting hole in the sink (be careful—don't kink the supply tubes). This type of faucet has mounting bolts that fit through the outside sink holes and secure the faucet with nuts and washers.

Note: Installation methods here call for a bead of silicone caulk between the faucet body and the sink. If your faucet comes with a rubber gasket, the caulk is unnecessary.

TOOLS
Common pliers and a basin wrench.

INSTALLING A NEW FAUCET WITH HOT AND COLD TAILPIECES

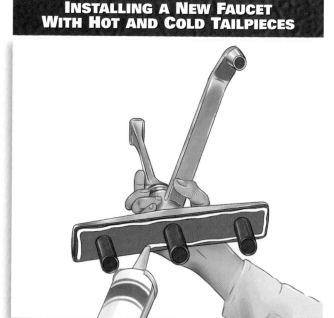

1 *Apply a bead of silicone caulk around the base of the faucet. Insert the faucet tailpieces into the openings in the sink. Make sure the faucet base is parallel to the back edge of the sink, then press down gently on the base to form a good seal. Wipe away excess caulk with a damp rag.*

2 *Under the sink, screw washers and mounting nuts onto the hot and cold water tailpieces. Tighten the nuts with pliers or a basin wrench. Make sure the faucet body is still parallel to the back edge of the sink. If it has shifted, loosen the mounting nuts and reposition the faucet. Then retighten the nuts.*

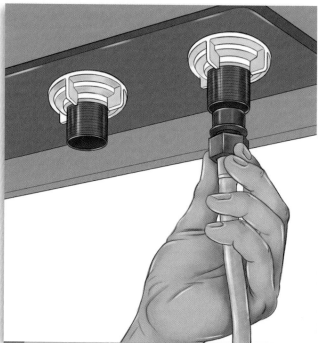

3 *Connect the tailpieces to the hot and cold water supply tubes under the sink, then connect the tubes to the shutoff valves.*

INSTALLING A NEW FAUCET WITH ATTACHED SUPPLY TUBES

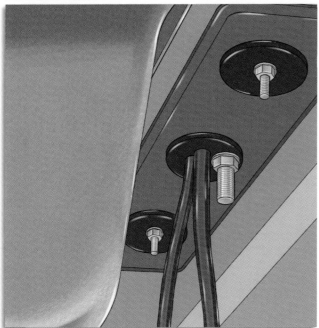

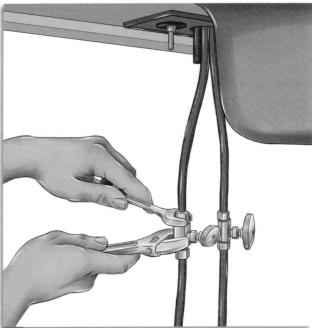

1 *Apply a bead of silicone caulk around the base of the faucet. Insert the copper supply tubes and center tailpiece into the center sink hole and the mounting bolts into the outside sink holes. Don't fold or kink the supply tubes. Make sure the faucet base is parallel to the back edge of the sink, then press down gently on the base to form a seal. Wipe away excess caulk with a damp rag.*

2 *From underneath the sink, place the washers and nuts onto the mounting bolts. Tighten the nuts with pliers or a basin wrench. Slip the retaining ring around the center tailpiece and the copper supply tubes and tighten the retaining nut. Attach the copper supply tubes to the plumbing supply shutoff valves.*

INSTALLING A SINK SPRAYER

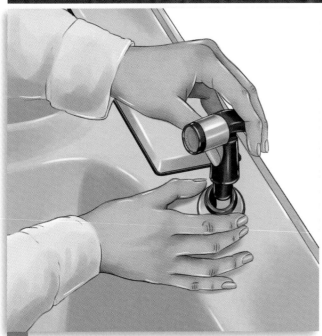

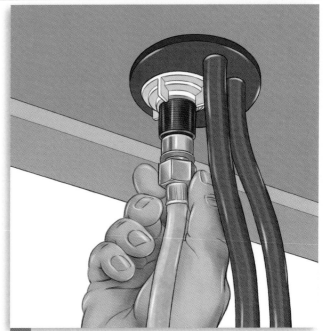

1 *Apply a bead of silicone caulk to the base of the sprayer. Insert the sprayer tailpiece into the sprayer sink hole. Press the base down firmly to form a good seal. Wipe away excess caulk with a damp rag.*

2 *From beneath the sink, place the washer and retaining nut onto the tailpiece. Tighten the nut with pliers or a basin wrench. Screw the sprayer hose onto the center tailpiece of the faucet.*

INSTALLING A GARBAGE DISPOSER

The switch for the disposer in this island counter is hidden behind a narrow, pull-out towel drawer.

Many kitchen sinks include a garbage disposer. However, some states and municipalities ban their use. If you are unsure, check with your local building authorities to see if you can install one.

A quality disposer has a ½-horsepower motor, a tank with a stainless steel interior, and sound insulation to ensure that it runs quietly. It should have a reversing motor that prevents jamming and a five-year warranty.

A disposer is either a batch-fed type, which means it runs only when the drain lid is in place, or it is a continuous-feed type, which allows you to add waste while the motor is running. Both types are attached to the sink drain system. Most codes require that the unit be plugged into a grounded outlet and that the outlet be controlled by an on-off switch. Usually, the on-off switch is located in the wall above the sink. A continuous-feed disposer attached to a sink in a peninsula or island cabinet may be controlled by a switch located inside a cabinet door to prevent the unit from being turned on accidentally.

Switches and outlets should be installed by an electrician. If the disposer requires attaching an electrical plug-in cord before installation, follow the manufacturer's directions carefully.

TOOLS

Flat-tip and Phillips-head screwdrivers, utility knife for cutting hoses, work light.

1 Apply a bead of silicone caulk under the edge of the drain opening sleeve. Insert the sleeve into the drain opening and press down to ensure a good seal. From underneath the sink, place the fiber gasket and backup ring onto the sleeve. Slip the lower mounting ring onto the sleeve and put the snap ring in place.

2 Hold the disposer against the lower mounting ring so that the lugs on the disposer line up with the mounting screws. Turn the mounting ring until the disposer is held firmly by the assembly.

3 Fasten the discharge tube to the discharge opening with the mounting washer.

4 If a dishwasher will be attached to the disposer unit, remove the plug from the dishwasher opening. Attach the dishwasher drain hose with a hose clamp.

5 Attach the drainpipe to the discharge tube with a slip nut and beveled washer. The bevel of the washer should face the threaded drainpipe.

6 Secure the disposer by inserting a screwdriver into the mounting lug located on the lower mounting ring. Tighten the mounting lug screw.

INSTALLING A RANGE HOOD

Aducted ventilation system eliminates cooking odors, excess water vapor, and smoke from the kitchen. The visible part of the system, the range hood, comes in styles to match any decor. More important than style, however, select a range hood with the proper capacity and size to fit your needs.

Range hoods use a fan to exhaust air to the outside of the house through vents. Vents are rated by the number of cubic feet of air per minute (CFM) that moves through them. For a hood that is mounted against a wall, the venting system should be rated at 450–650 CFM. For a hood mounted above a peninsula, the ratings should be 650–900 CFM. A hood over an island needs a CFM rating of 900–1,000. The depth of the hood, front to back, determines how far above the cooking surface the hood may be placed. A 16- to 17-inch hood should be no more than 21 inches from the cooktop; an 18- to 21-inch hood should be no more than 24 inches away; a 24-inch hood can be a maximum of 30 inches from the cooktop. At a minimum, the hood should equal the width of the cooking surface.

Range hood fans are either propeller-style or squirrel-cage type. The cylindrical squirrel-cage fan is quieter and more powerful but typically more expensive. The noise level of the fan is rated in units called sones. Choose a fan rated at eight sones or less.

Proper ducting determines whether an exhaust fan can work efficiently. The shortest, straightest route for vent ducts is best. Try to plan a location for the cooktop that will allow a range hood fan to be ducted directly out an adjacent exterior wall or through the roof. If ceiling joists run toward the wall where you wish to vent your system, you may be able to run ducts between joists to the outside. If not, you may be able to run the ducts through a soffit above the upper cabinets or through the upper portion of the upper cabinets themselves. The step-by-step instructions included here demonstrate how to install a vent hood between upper cabinets, but the instructions are adapted easily to a variety of situations.

Range hoods are hard-wired into your home's electrical system. Once you have determined a location for your range hood, have an electrician provide a 110-volt grounded electrical cable for your hood. You can make the final electrical connections yourself, but the electricity to the wire must be turned off at the circuit breaker panel before you proceed.

The range hood manufacturer will provide specifications for the maximum allowable duct length you can install. Keep in mind that each right angle turn is calculated as an additional 10 feet of duct length and that the number of turns is typically limited by building codes to a total of 180 degrees. Duct size also is specified, usually at 7 inches diameter for round ducting and $3\frac{1}{4}\times10$ inches for rectangular. Any ducts that pass through unheated areas, such as an attic, must be wrapped in fiberglass insulation.

Where the duct exits the house, you'll need to install a vent—either a wall cap, eave cap, or roof jack. These devices include a backdraft damper and a bug screen. Most house siding can be cut to provide an exit for a range hood ventilation system. The step-by-step instructions included here demonstrate how to cut a hole in brick.

A range hood nearly disappears behind a decorative panel made in the same style as the surrounding cabinets.

TOOLS

Measuring tape, drill equipped with power screwdriver tips, hand-held drywall saw, jigsaw, or reciprocating saw, utility knife, stud finder.

Tools for cutting masonry: masonry drill bits, cold chisel, ball peen hammer.

1 Position the hood liner between the cabinets, following the manufacturer's directions for the correct distance from the cooking surface. If necessary, install wooden shims between the liner and the cabinets to fill any space. Make sure that nails or screws are not long enough to penetrate into the cabinet interior.

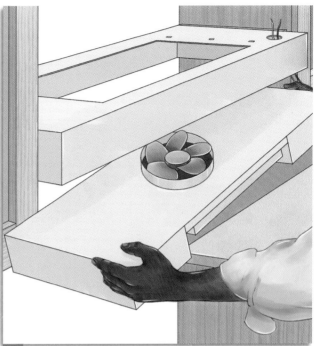

2 Remove all the access panels on the fan unit. Place the unit inside the liner and fasten in place with mounting bolts.

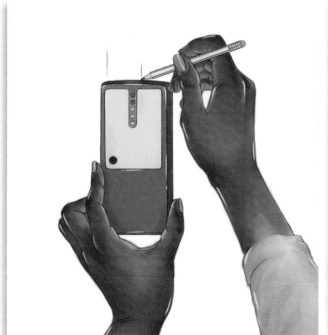

3 Use an electronic stud finder to locate wall studs. Mark location for vent duct on the wall surface. The exit hole should be about ½ inch larger than the diameter of the pipe.

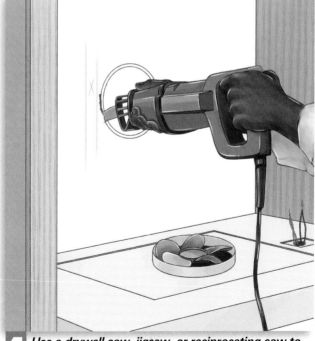

4 Use a drywall saw, jigsaw, or reciprocating saw to cut a hole in the drywall. Because this is an exterior wall, the cavity will be filled with insulation. Take care not to snag the saw blade on the insulation. After the hole is complete, use a utility knife to remove the insulation between the hole and the exterior sheathing.

INSTALLING A RANGE HOOD
continued

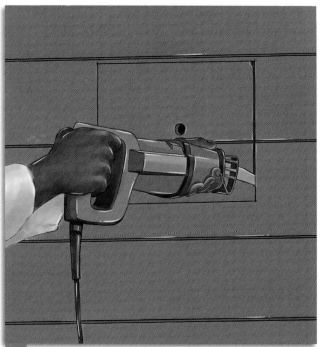

5 *Find the center of the duct hole, then transfer and mark this point on the inside surface of the exterior sheathing. Drill a pilot hole through the sheathing to the outside of the house. If your house exterior is clad with brick or other masonry, use a carbide-tipped masonry drill bit to make the pilot hole.*

6 *From outside, use the pilot hole as a center point to make an outline of the hole for the duct work. Cut the hole with a jigsaw or reciprocating saw. In masonry, drill a series of holes to trace the outline of the duct hole. Carefully remove the waste material using a cold chisel and ball peen hammer. Wear eye protection for this job.*

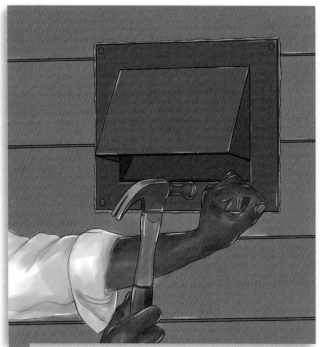

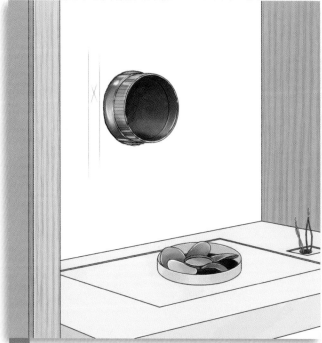

7 *Apply a bead of silicone caulk to the flange of the exterior duct cap. Center the cap in the hole and secure it to the exterior siding. If the siding is wood, metal, or vinyl, use sheet metal screws. If the siding is masonry, use 1½-inch masonry nails. Wipe away excess caulk with a damp rag.*

8 *From inside, slide a section of ductwork through the wall opening and onto the receiving end of the duct cap. Measure carefully from this point to determine the exact sizes of the remaining ductwork.*

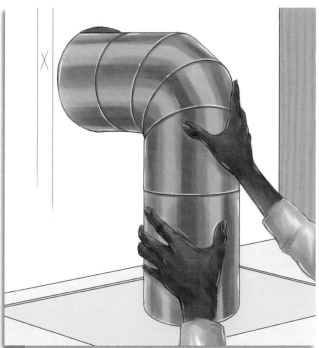

9 *Cut and fit ductwork between the range hood and the section attached to the exterior duct cap. At the range hood, drill several pilot holes where the duct fits over the range hood duct flange. Join the flange to the ductwork with ¾-inch sheet metal screws. Cover ductwork seams with duct tape.*

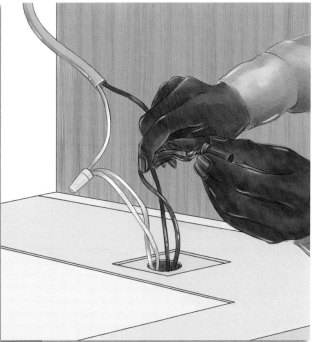

10 *Make sure electrical power to the circuit wire is shut off at the main circuit breaker panel. Hook the range hood's wires to the circuit wire. Use wire nuts to connect black wires to black, and white wires to white. Gently push the wires into the electrical junction box and replace all access panels.*

11 *Install any decorative panels over the fan unit. These generally are attached by screws into adjoining cabinets or the supporting wall.*

NOTE: *Some range hoods are mounted directly underneath an upper cabinet. Make the necessary cutouts in the bottom of the cabinet to allow space for the duct and to permit electrical connections.*

GLOSSARY

Adaptor. A fitting that joins pipes and other plumbing components not designed to connect directly.

Aerator. A device screwed into a faucet spout that mixes air with the flow of water to reduce splashing.

Basin wrench. Wrench designed to reach up behind a sink where other wrenches may not reach or have room to turn.

Basin wrench

Blocking. Lumber used to reinforce framing.

Coupling. A fitting that links two lengths of pipe in a straight run.

Crosscut. To saw wood across the pattern of its natural grain.

Drain-waste-vent (DWV) system. The network of pipes and fittings that convey wastes and gases out of a building.

Elbow. Also known as an ell, this fitting is used to change direction from one run of pipe to another.

Elbow

Fall. The slope of a drain line; minimum fall is ¼ inch per foot.

Fitting. Any pipe connector other than a valve.

Fixture. Any device that provides a flow of water or sanitary disposal of wastes. Examples include tubs, showers, sinks, and toilets.

Joists. Horizontal framing pieces that support a floor or ceiling.

Laminate. The process of applying a veneer. Also, a material formed of layers, such as plywood.

Ledger. Horizontal support for an end or edge of an assembly.

Main drain. That portion of the drainage system between fixture drains and the home's sewer drain.

Nippers. Tile-cutting hand tool for nibbling irregular shapes or small bits from ceramic tile.

Nippers

On-center (OC). Measurement from the center of one regularly spaced framing member to the next.

PVC. Polyvinyl chloride pipe, often used for cold water.

Plumber's putty. A pliable sealer often used around fixtures.

Reducer. A fitting with openings of different sizes used to connect one pipe to flow into a smaller one.

Rip. To saw wood parallel to its grain pattern.

Roughing-in. Initial plumbing, carpentry, and electrical work.

Run. A line of pipes or cabinets.

Scribing strip. Top edge of a backsplash, designed to be cut to conform to irregularities in the wall.

Scribing strip

Sheet goods. Plywood and similar materials produced as panels. Also, flooring installed in sheets.

Shim. Wedging thin materials (shims) under or behind surfaces to make them level or plumb.

Spackle. A paste that dries and can be sanded after application. It fills cracks and holes in walls.

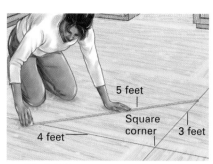

"3-4-5" test to verify square

Square. Lines or surfaces forming a 90-degree angle. Test by using the "3-4-5" method, above: Measure along one side of the angle and mark a point 3 feet from the corner. Mark a point 4 feet from the corner along the other side. If the diagonal measurement between these points is 5 feet, the corner is square.

Stile. A vertical section of a cabinet facing.

Tailpiece. Short drainpipe between a fixture drain and a trap. Also, the inlet tubes on a faucet that connect it to water supply lines.

Trap. A bend in a drainpipe that creates a water seal to prevent sewer gases from escaping through fixtures.

Undercut. Saw technique for removing the bottoms of door frames to make room for tile or other high-profile flooring.

Undercut

Vent. A piping route by which gases leave a building's plumbing system.

Wet wall. A wall framed to enclose a building's main drain/vent stack, water lines, and DWV lines.

Wire nut. Threaded plastic caps that splice electrical wires and protect splices or exposed wire ends.

Wire nut

INDEX

Numbers in italic type indicate pages with photographs or illustrations related to the topic.

METRIC CONVERSIONS

U.S. Units to Metric Equivalents			Metric Units to U.S. Equivalents		
To Convert From	Multiply By	To Get	To Convert From	Multiply By	To Get
Inches	25.4	Millimetres	Millimetres	0.0394	Inches
Inches	2.54	Centimetres	Centimetres	0.3937	Inches
Feet	30.48	Centimetres	Centimetres	0.0328	Feet
Feet	0.3048	Metres	Metres	3.2808	Feet
Yards	0.9144	Metres	Metres	1.0936	Yards
Square inches	6.4516	Square centimetres	Square centimetres	0.1550	Square inches
Square feet	0.0929	Square metres	Square metres	10.764	Square feet
Square yards	0.8361	Square metres	Square metres	1.1960	Square yards
Acres	0.4047	Hectares	Hectares	2.4711	Acres
Cubic inches	16.387	Cubic centimetres	Cubic centimetres	0.0610	Cubic inches
Cubic feet	0.0283	Cubic metres	Cubic metres	35.315	Cubic feet
Cubic feet	28.316	Litres	Litres	0.0353	Cubic feet
Cubic yards	0.7646	Cubic metres	Cubic metres	1.308	Cubic yards
Cubic yards	764.55	Litres	Litres	0.0013	Cubic yards

To convert from degrees Fahrenheit (F) to degrees Celsius (C), first subtract 32, then multiply by $\frac{5}{9}$.

To convert from degrees Celsius to degrees Fahrenheit, multiply by $\frac{9}{5}$, then add 32.